COUNSELLING FOR YOUNG PEOPLE

· COUNSELLING IN CONTEXT ·

Series editors
Moira Walker and Michael Jacobs
University of Leicester

Counselling takes place in many different contexts: in voluntary and statutory agencies; in individual private practice or in a consortium; at work, in medical settings, in churches and in different areas of education. While there may be much in common in basic counselling methods (despite theoretical differences), each setting gives rise to particular areas of concern, and often requires specialist knowledge, both of the problems likely to be brought, but also of the context in which the client is being seen. Even common counselling issues vary slightly from situation to situation in the way they are applied and understood.

This series examines eleven such areas, and applies a similar scheme to each, first looking at the history of the development of counselling in that particular context; then at the context itself, and how the counsellor fits into it. Central to each volume are chapters on common issues related to the specific setting and questions that may be peculiar to it but could be of interest and value to counsellors working elsewhere. Each book will provide useful information for anyone considering counselling, or the provision of counselling in a particular context. Relationships with others who work in the same setting whether as counsellors, managers or administrators are also examined; and each book concludes with the author's own critique of counselling as it is currently practised in that context.

Current and forthcoming titles

COUNSELLING FOR YOUNG PEOPLE

Judith Mabey
and Bernice Sorensen

OPEN UNIVERSITY PRESS
Buckingham · Philadelphia

Open University Press
Celtic Court
22 Ballmoor
Buckingham
MK18 1XW

and
1900 Frost Road, Suite 101
Bristol, PA 19007, USA

First Published 1995
Reprinted 1996

A catalogue record of this book is available from the British Library

ISBN 0 335 19298 X (pb)

Library of Congress Cataloging-in-Publication Data
Mabey, Judith A.
Counselling for young people / by Judith Mabey and Bernice
Sorensen.
p.   cm. — (Counselling in context)
Includes bibliographical references and index.
ISBN 0–335–19298–X (pbk.)
1. Youth—Counselling of—Great Britain. I. Sorensen, Bernice.
II. Title. III. Series.
HV1441.G7M33   1995
362.7'1—dc20   94–41293
CIP

Typeset by Graphicraft Typesetters Ltd, Hong Kong
Printed in Great Britain by St Edmundsbury Press,
Bury St Edmunds, Suffolk

This book is dedicated, with love, to the memory of our friend and colleague Dee Bristow, who died on 16 October 1993 just before her fiftieth birthday. She was much loved and is greatly missed.

Deep peace of the running wave to you
Deep peace of the silent stars to you
Deep peace of the flowing air to you
Deep peace of the quiet earth to you
May peace fill your soul
Let peace make you whole
(Celtic blessing)

Goodbye Dee, and thank you.

Contents

Series editors' preface

When the older generation complains about adolescents, that they are not as they were in their own younger days, there is a feeling of *déjà vu*. Did not they hear the same sentiment expressed by their elders? Young people have always been portrayed in the same way, from generation to generation, as pre-occupied with self, with each other, and with knocking the world around them. In fact they need a period of relative freedom, of being able to be immature, although in present day society this is an increasingly problematic and complex time.

Such a picture of perennial adolescence, flowering every year as each cohort reaches the teenage or pubertal watershed has some truth in it. But there may be differences in Britain amongst those who have come to be called 'Thatcher's children'. Many of that age group have not had the opportunities to experiment within a secure framework: unemployment amongst young people means that far too many have been excluded from the hope that employment or apprenticeship brings. They are living in an increasingly materialistic and consumer-driven society that values money and possessions over people, and measures acceptability and status by what you have rather than by what you are. The higher education option may be taken up by more young people (who for at least those three or four years of their degree will have a sense of purpose); but they are now under great financial stresses. That particular group are discussed specifically in another book in this series on counselling in further and higher education. This volume focuses on the younger age group and those who have not entered tertiary education.

The importance of separate services for these young people has long been acknowledged: their needs are distinct and related to a particular stage of their development. As Winnicott said, young people may be very interested in psychological ideas, but they do not want to apply the ideas too deeply to themselves. They want to remain separate, even on their own, and find their own way. They need services that will respond to their particular needs and see them quickly: for some, because today's disaster is tomorrow's nonchalance; and for others because they face problems of such enormous magnitude that they cannot face them alone, and cannot tolerate them any longer. They need counsellors who can be flexible and adaptable and who have a real understanding of, and empathy with, young people. They need people who can understand but who do not condescend, patronize or pass judgement.

Judith Mabey and Bernice Sorensen draw upon all their experience of working with young people to identify the issues, and to illustrate the possibilities and the problems of counselling young people. The projects they refer to are marked by the creativity and the tremendous energy and commitment of those who work in them, both as volunteers and as paid workers. They all too often struggle against a lack of resources. It is of course a truism to say that these services are working with our future, but it is nonetheless worth stating. If in this day and age we cannot help those who need to make what can be a difficult transition from childhood to the raw realities of the adult world, we are failing in an important task. There is a danger of sacrificing young people to the political and societal whims of what sometimes looks like a heartless older generation.

Moira Walker
Michael Jacobs

Acknowledgements

We began writing this book with great trepidation and would never have believed how much we have subsequently enjoyed doing it. We have received a great deal of help and support from many quarters and are delighted to be able to acknowledge some of them now.

Most important of all we want to thank our families, Jens and Elise Sorensen and Mike, Brendan and Iyabo Mabey for tolerating the intrusion into their lives. Our friend and tame computer expert, Gerald Parker, saved us from insanity on several occasions when the Amstrads refused to do what we asked them to: we do appreciate his help. Three wonderful women, Jane Dawson, Val Hill and Sheilagh Jevons gave us loads of support and encouragement on our weekends together.

We want to thank our editors Moira Walker and Michael Jacobs for their wisdom and patience and for being so responsive to us. Many individuals and agencies responded to our requests for information and opinions and without their help this would have been a thin volume. We want to extend our special thanks to: Tony Hurst, Denny Rablah, John Sivyer, Pete Francis, Arthur Musgrave, Helen Thompson, Eileen McDonald, Alison McKay, Hazel Lamb, Malcolm Phillips, Dick Saxton, Alan Jamieson, John Towler, Tim Bond, Sue Hughs, Elizabeth Aspinall and Mike Hockings.

The following projects and agencies all deserve our thanks and appreciation: JAC (Utrecht, the Netherlands), Mancroft Advice, Yakeen, Time Out, Centre 33, Off the Record, the Child Advocacy Project, Relateteen, Alateen and most of all, Signpost. The co-ordinators of many young people's agencies were also helpful to us and we do appreciate their contributions.

When we finished this book we were left with a feeling of admiration and a great desire to acknowledge and celebrate the excellent work and commitment of so many people who give their time, expertise and energy to providing services to young people. They struggle to cope with ever-diminishing resources on the one hand and ever-increasing demand on the other. They continue to do this work because they appreciate and believe in young people, with all their idealism and challenge. They know that these services are worth fighting for. We were also left feeling angry and frustrated at the lack of resources, support and encouragement that this work receives. What kind of a statement is being made about the value of young people in our society? We can only hope for a change in political will that will bring about investment in young people, our most precious resource for the future.

We would like to end these acknowledgements by thanking all the young clients we have worked with over the years, for what they have taught us, for the inspiration and challenge they have given us, and for keeping our feet on the ground and our egos in check.

· ONE ·

The development of
counselling for young people

YOUNG PEOPLE IN POST-WAR BRITAIN

Among the many social changes that have taken place in post-war Britain has been the emergence of adolescence as an identifiable stage in personal development, with its own recognizable set of problems and difficulties for the individual and society specific to this stage in life.

The period immediately after the Second World War was marked by economic expansion and full employment. The young families of those who had returned from fighting were growing up in a world with ever-expanding horizons. There was a rush to increase both public and private housing stock by extensive building programmes. By the early to mid-fifties television was finding its way into many homes. Most young people leaving school could confidently expect to find their way on to one of the increasing number of apprentice-ship schemes as their passport into the world of work. By the late fifties and early sixties the shortfall in available labour for manual jobs was being met by the immigration programme, bringing men and women from parts of the shrinking empire to work and set up home in the 'mother country'.

At the same time the phenomenon called 'youth culture' was emerging. In the United States young actors like James Dean and Marlon Brando were presenting images of young people as dis-turbed and angry, misunderstood by and alienated from their par-ents and elders, whose moral and ethical values they challenged and rejected. Courting danger and excitement, their highly sexualized images were very threatening to the society of the day, even though they were irresistibly attractive to the young. These conficts were explored in films like *Rebel Without a Cause*.

In the music world, the gyrating hips of Elvis Presley were causing consternation, while he, together with Buddy Holly, the Big
Bopper and many others were popularizing rock and roll. This music,
with its roots in black rhythm and blues, was sweeping across
America and Europe. In Britain it was danced to by the Teddy boys
and girls. Young men sported brightly coloured drainpipe trousers
with matching long line jackets and crêpe-soled shoes while their
girlfriends favoured backcombed, bouffant hairstyles, bright lipstick
and full skirts.

Economic prosperity and full employment meant that young
people found themselves in possession of disposable income, which
quickly brought them to the attention of the music, entertainment
and fashion industries. The 'teenager' as a consumer was born.
Young people, perhaps for the first time, were bombarded with
messages about how to look, how to dress, what music to listen to,
what to smoke or chew and generally how to be. These messages
were reinforced by peer pressure and sealed by the reaction to
parental disapproval. One way to create an identity was to be different. Of course this in itself was not a new phenomenon, the
bright young things and the flappers of the twenties and thirties
had had the same idea and had met with the same cocktail of
parental concern and disapproval, but they had been predominantly
upper-class socialites.

By the early sixties a youth culture was firmly established. The
rise to fame of the Beatles ensured that its epicentre was no longer
the United States, but Britain. Beatle suits and haircuts were the
height of fashion. The Mersey beat emanating from Liverpool was
being answered by groups like the Rolling Stones and the Who
from the south and the Animals from the north east. As the sixties
progressed, reports emerged of gangs of young people divided into
Mods wearing parka jackets and riding scooters and Rockers, riding
motorcycles and wearing leathers, who were engaging in long-
running battles in British seaside towns. Women's skirts were
becoming shorter and men's hair longer. London's Carnaby Street
was the centre of youth fashion and Mary Quant and Biba became
household names.

From the USA came the phenomenon that was to be known as
the 'protest movement'. Following in the footsteps of Woody Guthrie,
a young man called Bob Dylan was writing songs about social issues. Reading poetry and wearing black polo neck sweaters became
all the rage. Donovan, often held up as Britain's answer to Dylan,
was a good deal less earnest and perhaps more melodic. The interest
in poetry was furthered by the emergence of the Mersey beat poets.

A well-fingered book of poetry became an essential fashion acces-sory in sixth forms and colleges all over Britain.

At the same time, as the contraceptive pill became more widely available, giving women much greater control over their fertility, patterns of sexual behaviour and attitudes were beginning to change. Sex outside of marriage was no longer considered a disgraceful activity and young people found themselves faced with a whole new set of moral dilemmas about their relationships.

Two other significant factors in the sixties were the opposition to the Vietnam war, which politicized many young people, who by the late 1960s were being enfranchised for the first time at 18. The expansion of the drug culture encouraged young people to (in the words of drug guru Timothy Leary) 'turn on' to drugs. The alterna-tive culture provided by radical politics helped them to 'tune in' to new ideas, music, and ways of life. There was also a 'drop out' from education and conventional society, with its outmoded morality.

Education was not exempt from the general liberalization that took place in the sixties. The old ideas of teaching the three Rs, reinforced if necessary by means of the cane, were being replaced with the concept of 'child-centred' education, where a programme of learning was built around the individual needs of the child, rather than the child being required to merely fit into present educational norms. This brought about the virtual disappearance of streaming within primary schools and coincided with the introduction of the comprehensive system of secondary education. In time there was an expansion of personal and social education in the curriculum and of the pastoral care system within schools.

The raising of the school leaving age to 16 meant that considerable thought had to be given to the kind of curriculum that would be appropriate, particularly for those young people who were neither academic nor motivated. But, as is most often the case with educa-tional reform, the additional funding made available was, at best, minimal.

In the late sixties and early seventies 'flower power' had spread from the USA to Britain. The 1969 Woodstock festival had really crystallized this movement, characterized by its optimism, its drug culture, its anti-materialism, its radical politics and its music. Icons included Jimi Hendrix from America and Cream and Pink Floyd from Britain. Long hair, long clothes, flowers and psychedelia abounded. The Beatles, no longer wearing suits, brought out their *Magical Mystery Tour* album. Films like *Easy Rider* explored the con-flicts between the new thinking and old ways. The Portobello Road market replaced Carnaby Street as *the* place to shop. Student halls smelt of joss sticks and marijuana. The babyboomers had become hippies.

In Britain some, mainly working-class, young people reacted against the 'love and peace' philosophy of the hippies. They became skinheads, so called because of their close-cropped hair. They wore utilitarian, neat and clean but rather ugly clothes and their predisposition to violence meant that they were also known as bootboys or bovverboys. They listened to Jamaican Ska music and their rather regimented style of dancing contrasted strongly with the free style of the hippies.

By the early seventies, the immigrant communities that had been growing through the sixties were well established in towns and cities – Britain was fast becoming a multiracial society. In addition to the inner-city poverty and deprivation that they shared with their white neighbours, the black and Asian communities and their young people, many of whom were by now second and third generation, had to cope with the inherent and widespread racism of British society and its institutions. Black and Asian youth found themselves having to straddle two profoundly different and often uncompromising cultures with the terrible possibility of being alienated from and rejected by both.

In the seventies, the popularization of the Women's Movement in Britain, with its challenges to traditional gender roles and previously accepted norms, although undoubtedly beneficial, brought with it new stresses to women themselves, to men and to young people. However heinous and unfair the previously accepted roles were, both men and women knew where they were. Since the seventies women have found themselves under pressure to achieve academically and in their careers, while remaining slim, young and beautiful and ensuring that domestic duties and child care carry on to the same standard as ever. Men have found their authority challenged and their bastions of power and privilege under siege. Their response has included, at one end of the continuum, the emergence of the often emasculated 'new man', and at the other, the increase in violence against women in almost every sphere. Inevitably young people of both genders are left struggling with how they should themselves react amidst all this confusion.

The mid- to late seventies were a low point in popular music. Bands from earlier days were still around but many of them had grown very wealthy and were almost establishment figures. 'Middle of the road' music was around but the irrepressible idealism of the young was soon to re-emerge with the punk explosion. This movement was a reaction to what many young people perceived as the taking over of youth culture by big business, both in the music and fashion worlds. The aim was to return youth culture to the streets. Young people wore black plastic bin bags held together by safety pins. Hundreds of punk bands sprung up all over the country, many of whom are best remembered by their enthusiasm rather than their talent. Hair was spiked and dyed bright colours. Youth culture had regained its edge.

Thatcherism, in the eighties, brought about a revolution in social attitudes that should not be underestimated. The idealism of the sixties and the liberalization of the seventies gave way to a hard-nosed individualism which denied the value of the whole concept of society and replaced it with an 'every man for himself' mentality. As cost cutting and rationalization became the watchwords, job security became a thing of the past. The systematic dismantlement of the manufacturing base of British industry in favour of the service industries meant a massive reduction in apprenticeship schemes. This, together with the recession, caused a huge increase in youth unemployment.

Social policy changes that stressed individual and family responsibility had the effect of removing the social security safety net from under many young people and led to an increase in poverty and homelessness among the young. In addition, the change in public attitudes on individual responsibility and the re-emergence of notions of the 'feckless' poor, responsible for their own plight, has added the blight of a sense of failure and worthlessness to the practical problems experienced by many of the young.

Dangerous ambivalence about sex education, particularly concerning the issue of homosexuality in the young was a spin-off of the desire to return to the so-called 'Victorian family values'. This had found its voice in the eighties, just at the time when the spread of HIV infection made it imperative that young people be as knowledgeable as possible in order to make informed choices and to be aware of safer sexual practices. Despite the best efforts of the 'Moral Majority' and the infamous Clause 28, which legislated against the 'promotion' of homosexuality thus making its inclusion in sex education problematic, organizations like the Terence Higgins Trust made valiant and concerted efforts to inform, advise and support young people in their choices. However, as a result of the sensationalist and biased media coverage and lacklustre governmental response to the health crisis posed by the spread of HIV, there has been a rise in homophobia and a vilification of drug users. This has had serious ramifications for many young people.

Youth culture did not remain untouched by the technological

revolution that gathered momentum in the eighties, with its home computers and video games. Black American styles of dress began appearing on British streets and personal stereos vibrated to the beat of rap music. The dance craze was for robotics and break dancing. Young men in particular were seen demonstrating their athletic and artistic prowess on street corners. Reggae, another form of Jamaican music, always popular with the black community, became more widely listened to.

The materialism of the eighties was reflected by the popularization of designer wear for the young. Labels and brand names became all-important. Fitness became a fashion and designer sports wear, which cost a fortune, was worn by most young people, even those whose greatest sporting achievement was getting out of bed in the morning. The eighties, which had begun ominously with the assassination of John Lennon, ended with the proliferation of the ghastly shell suit.

And so to the nineties, where many young people find themselves in crisis, facing the worst youth unemployment since the war. They are members of a society with a suspect ideology which, on the one hand, acknowledges and decries the breakdown of the family, and on the other hand, refuses to care for or realistically support the young people who can easily become the flotsam and jetsam of family storms. Society often equates worth with wealth and status, or with colour, gender and sexual preference. It expects young people to grow up and find their way in the world while offering them minimum support and maximum censure. It was never easy to be an adolescent, but we may ask whether in present society it has been made more difficult than ever before.

ADOLESCENCE

The Oxford English Dictionary defines 'adolescence' as:

> The process or condition of growing up; the growing age of human beings; the period which extends from childhood to manhood or womanhood; youth; ordinarily considered as extending from 14 to 25 in males, and from 12 to 21 in females.

For the purposes of this work, we define 'young people' as those between the ages of 13 and 25, including therefore those in the upper age range, whose physical, mental, educational or social development would tend to ally them more with others chronologically younger than themselves.

During the period of human development that we call adolescence, a young person must progress from childhood to adulthood and from dependency to independence and autonomy. There are many similarities between this transition and the process of individuation that happens in early childhood, during which the child learns to see herself as a person physically and psychologically separate from, and yet dependent on, the mother or primary care provider.

Just as the successful conclusion of this early process in human development is dependent on a mother's willingness to allow a child to move out of the symbiotic relationship towards individuation, so in adolescence a successful conclusion of the process requires a parent or carer to recognize, allow and facilitate a young person's need to move out of the dependent role of a child in the family towards independence, autonomy and maturity.

Children introject the social and moral values and ways of behaving of their families. Adolescents begin to question this imposed value system and it becomes more important to be in line with their peers than with their parents. This is part of their search for an identity and a value system that is their own. The shift is from being part of a family group, to being part of a peer group and to standing alone as an adult.

For many young people the need to belong to a recognizable peer group with some level of common ideology and group identity is paramount. This need is related not only to the general human search for friendship and companionship but rather to a much more profound need for security and acceptability. Peer groups at this stage of life provide much-needed support and reassurance at a time of turbulence and uncertainty, and both expect and extract fierce loyalty from the young people who make up the membership. Herein lies the explanation for the intolerance of, and hostility towards, those on the outside of the group as well as what could otherwise be construed as fanaticism on the part of the young.

During adolescence, young people undergo rapid and radical physiological changes. As well as the increase in height and strength, the onset of puberty brings sexual development. This is a period fraught with anxiety for most young people. There is considerable difference in the rate of growth and sexual development in any group of adolescents and, wherever they are on the continuum, they can feel awkward and out of step with their peers and with their sex. Sexual awareness and interest is high at this stage in life and with it anxiety about appearance can become almost obsessional.

In addition they are having to make value judgements about their sexual behaviour and activity.

For some young people issues around sexual preference may become a focus of concern. Consistent attraction to and interest in people of the same gender as themselves may make them feel out of step with their peers. The ramifications of their sexual preference, in a homophobic society, may well give rise to anxiety.

The education system in Britain, and indeed in most of the developed world, is organized in such a way that during this period of emotional and physical turbulence young people are faced with a set of educational hoops through which they must jump. Their future prospects depend upon the examination system. For some this comes when they are least able to cope with it because their priorities lie not with school work but with peer group activities.

As they seek to define themselves, the inner world of the adolescent is often fraught with struggle and conflict. The certainties of childhood have been removed. They are faced with the shifting sands of physical, emotional, sexual and intellectual growth and development, in a familial, social and political context packed with paradox and mixed messages.

The stresses, difficulties and dangers inherent in this transition from childhood to adulthood are myriad. Some are focused on relationships within the family, others on the young person's acceptability to, or isolation from, peer groups. Others involve their ability to succeed academically or to get and keep a job. Finally they may be concerned with their relationship with themselves and their emerging sense of themselves as part of society.

YOUNG PEOPLE IN EDUCATION

Counselling in the sphere of education grew out of what is loosely termed 'guidance' which developed in the early 1900s. Milner (1980) states that in the past the term 'guidance' in education

> has mainly been used to describe three distinct and restrictive activities – Child Guidance, often provided by a medical service; vocational guidance, provided by the new Careers Service, and educational guidance, provided mainly by the School Psychological Service.
>
> (Milner 1980: 25)

Under the terms of the 1910 Education Act, local education authorities were asked to arrange to help young people, up to the age of 17, in their choice of employment. The Youth Employment Service, set up as a result of the 1948 Employment and Training Act, provided 'vocational guidance' to young people, including school leavers, up to the age of 18. These services were superseded in 1973 by a new Careers Service.

'Educational guidance' is offered through the School Psychological Service by educational psychologists. Much of the work is confined to attainment testing for the purpose of streaming and selection for the eleven-plus age group. Even with the demise of that examination, educational psychologists have been more concerned with assessment and administering and interpreting standard tests of ability.

Alongside these developments, 'Child Guidance' clinics were established in 1921. These were medical rather than educational, and they offered a service to children 'of normal intelligence' whose behaviour in some way was seen to be problematic or disruptive. However, these developments were happening outside of the school environment. School counselling emerged, not through education, but as a result of the recommendations of the National Association for Mental Health at a conference held in 1963:

> School counselling is one outcome of the intention to improve the quality of schools as caring institutions with a responsibility for maintaining, protecting and promoting the personal development and well-being of children . . . Counselling in schools is basically a 'preventive' mental health service.
>
> (Milner 1980: 26)

This idea of prevention was an important theme throughout the next stages of the development of counselling in schools. The first courses in counselling and guidance were set up at Reading and Keele universities in 1965. They were influenced by similar courses offered in American universities and were firmly based on the works of Carl Rogers, thus offering a person-centred, non-directive view of education, with the added American dimension of developmental and behavioural counselling.

Another factor which enabled the growth of counselling in schools was the emergence of comprehensive education. These larger schools, with greater course choice and flexibility had the resources to employ staff, either full- or part-time, to carry out counselling and guidance activities.

By 1966 a national association was created as a result of the meeting of a number of mature students from the Reading and Keele courses: they formed the National Association of Educational Counsellors. This was essentially a support group who met and focused on such issues as vocational guidance, group counselling, counsellor training etc. It was renamed the National Association of Counsellors in Education (NACE) and it aimed to establish a professional code of ethics, disseminate ideas and research findings and establish contact with other organizations in sympathy with their aims and objectives. It was proposed that NACE would form the basis of a new division in the British Association for Counselling (BAC), formerly The Standing Conference for the Advancement of Counselling, which is an umbrella organization with various divisions or associations that represent different areas of counselling. In 1970 a new group formed, called the Association of Student Counsellors. It aimed to provide a professional organization for those involved in counselling young people. These included students in tertiary colleges as well as those in Further and Higher Education. Like NACE it also became a division of BAC.

In the 1970s a flowering of counselling was taking place in schools. However, by the eighties things had changed. A shift took place from specialist counselling roles to a system where more and more teachers were valuing basic counselling skills, and using them in a pastoral setting. This was paralleled in the report of The European Community Action Programme (1985) which stated that guidance and counselling should not be a separate activity imposed on the normal fabric of the school, but an integral part of its curriculum. This change from the practice of the seventies led to an emphasis on educational and vocational counselling and a move away from personal counselling.

What caused this change in emphasis from the seventies to the eighties? Hooper and Lang wrote in an article in *Pastoral Care*:

> Most of those who have been involved in education since the seventies are conscious that there have been significant changes in relation to counsellors and counselling . . . few have a clear idea of the nature and extent of these changes. The key factors that many will have some knowledge of are the apparent decrease in full-time counsellor posts, and the closing of a number of major full-time counselling courses.
>
> (Hooper and Lang 1988: 28)

Research published in 1977 reported that there were 351 counsellors working within the school system in England and Wales, although 54 per cent of them were employed in only nine education authorities (Antournis 1977). By 1987 there were only 90 counsellors; 28 were employed by the Devon Education Authority, 11 at Dudley, 6 in Leicestershire, 4 in Oxfordshire. Rotherham and the ILEA still supported counselling but no specific numbers were available (Hooper and Lang 1988).

Law's research in 1977, involving 400 teachers and counsellors, highlighted two opposing orientations: the 'system orientation', which he uses to describe counsellors who 'see themselves as acting on behalf of the organization in which they work' and an 'open orientation' with counsellors 'whose objectives have more to do with personal freedom than with adjustment to socially imposed roles' (Law 1975: 81–90). The former are more concerned with the pupil in the context of the school environment, and favour behaviour-modification techniques. The latter accept the possibility of a young person's opposition to the demands of the school and favour a person-centred model.

These are important differences and reflect changing cultural attitudes. The 'open orientation' reflects the individualism of the sixties, a time, as we have seen, when young people became a force to be reckoned with, even if it was from a mainly commercial viewpoint. By the eighties, with the rise of Thatcherism, there was a move away from this emphasis to the personal development of the individual. In the schools, more emphasis was placed upon the development of a school curriculum which would, on the one hand, produce students with competences more suited to the perceived needs of industry, and on the other, enable students to feel they were getting a more relevant education.

In the dwindling job market there were less and less opportunities for unskilled labour, so greater emphasis was placed on achievement. Academic success was seen to be increasingly necessary if young people were to enter the employment market. Opposition to, or rebellion against the demands of the school, on the part of a student now became tantamount to a refusal to move towards taking adult responsibility. Ironically, as the number of real jobs available to young people diminished, long-term, unavoidable unemployment became the most likely prospect for many young people.

PREVENTIVE OR REMEDIAL COUNSELLING?

The prophylactic or preventive role of the counsellor was emphasized from the beginning (NAMH 1970), Daws (1973: 2) summing this up as 'pupil-focused' work, offered to children in crisis, or to vulnerable and deviant children. Other children are seen only for educational and vocational reasons. 'Environment-focused work'

within the school is with 'irascible' teachers, and 'disturbed' families
rather than with the children. These are not in reality preventative
measures but remedial. Preventive work is only done through 'guid-
ing' teams of colleagues, in both pastoral work and a personal and
social setting. As Law concludes:

> There is a real danger that the prophylactic role of the coun-
> sellor has been so widely emphasized and disseminated that
> the minimal sense in which most counsellors serve preventa-
> tive ends (a situation unlikely to change very much) will go
> unrecognized.
>
> (Law 1975: 85)

Thus there has been a move away from personal counselling to
a more co-ordinated educational and vocational approach, with an
emphasis on preventive work, but rarely with the resources to follow
it through in any genuinely comprehensive way. Maguire (1975)
argues strongly that the developmental model of counselling ex-
pounded by the early courses in counselling and guidance deals
primarily with the normal child. Some counsellors deal with the
so-called 'problem children' in schools, where it is recognized that
the expertise of the counsellor is perhaps better used. Responding
to these needs is felt to be more useful than undertaking guidance
duties which can be effectively handled by teachers with less specialized training.

Jones's research in 1975 estimated that 14 per cent of children
have symptoms of emotional disturbance and maladjustment. This
includes 1 to 2 per cent who have severe psychiatric disturbance
necessitating psychomedical attention. However, over the last twenty-
five years, there has been a decrease in the provision of psychological and psychiatric services to children. Hence Maguire (1975)
strongly supports the case for the employment of trained and specialist therapeutic counsellors to meet the needs of this 14 per cent
of children, including those who would not currently receive help
from the available specialist services.

Obviously there are training and funding implications in this type
of recommendation. However, the advantages of having a therapeutic counsellor available within the school are threefold. First,
having specialist help on site removes the dilemma as to whether
or not to refer children to outside agencies at the first stage. Second,
it is likely to be more acceptable to parents, who might not favour
referrals to outside agencies such as the Child Guidance clinics.
Finally, it prevents the labelling that outside referrals inevitably
cause. An inside specialist can work more closely with the young

person within the school setting and be available to staff to support their everyday work with troubled pupils.

In the eighties we have traced a move from more specialist counselling services to a greater emphasis on educational and vocational services. However, this has not meant a lack of interest in counselling or counselling skills, rather a change in emphasis.

CONTEMPORARY COUNSELLING IN SCHOOLS

In the seventies and early eighties the word 'counselling' was relatively unused in a school setting. Today it is frequently used but the meanings attached to it are very varied. For example, it may be used to denote crisis conversations, general advice-giving, career interviews, informal pupil–teacher discussions or discipline-linked interviews. The eighties and early nineties have seen an increased commitment to pastoral care systems co-ordinated by year heads and their team of year tutors. More recognition is given to the need for all young people to have access to at least informal counselling during stages of difficulty which most are likely to experience at some time in their school career.

Murgatroyd speaks of an increase in demand for counselling at this time because 'there is a great deal of frustration, anxiety, stress and distress' (1983: 43). The majority of teachers today would support the usefulness of counselling skills. Counselling courses have teachers well represented in their numbers and schools increasingly offer in-service counselling training days. For example, one school in Middlesex engaged counsellor trainers to look at counselling with each year-group team, to see how tutors could use these skills within their tutor group. They were helped to recognize the different issues students have at the different stages of development, and the different responses required.

Trained specialist school counsellors are now so rare that work with disturbed children is mostly referred to young persons' counselling agencies. Mosely concludes in her article, 'Is There a Place for Counselling in Schools?':

> We live in troubled times; with high unemployment, schools often seem irrelevant places and the problems and the tasks of childhood and adolescence are exacerbated even further. It is crucial we can offer counselling as a positive force in pupils' lives; not as a 'safety net' nor as an unwitting form of social control but as a means of helping young people think

for themselves, make their own decisions, value their own
integrity.

(Mosely 1993: 105)

She advocates carefully run peer group counselling, ideally alongside an individual counselling facility. Does this reflect a renewed
call for a return to a more specialist service, with a recognition of
the usefulness of group work? It will be interesting to see where
increasing teacher awareness for the need for counselling skills leads.

COUNSELLING YOUNG PEOPLE IN THE COMMUNITY

The last decades have seen a variety of social and legislative changes
that have affected young people. The response to these has depended
in part on who has been involved in the setting up of services,
whether it has been young people, adults, professionals, voluntary
groups etc. What emerges from an overview of agencies that have
been established over the last 30 years is a tremendous difference
of approaches and hence a diversity in the types of services offered
to young people.

In the 1960s workers from both the Youth Service and Marriage
Guidance (now Relate) identified a gap in services provided for
young people, in respect of information, advice and counselling.
Lawton (1985: 40) distinguishes three main strands of development
that followed: the first was to make 'Marriage Guidance-style therapeutic and remedial counselling' services available to young people.
The second was the development of services set up by young people
which offered practical information and advice, as well as emotional support. Third, existing professional services were made more
accessible to young people, for example, those offering contraception and psychotherapy.

In the 1970s both the Youth Service and to a lesser extent, the
Social Services, became involved with promoting information, advice, social education and counselling. Like Marriage Guidance, these
services already had a tradition of using volunteers, and this trend
continued to be embraced and broadened by the influence of Citizens Advice Bureaux and the Samaritans, the latter adding befriending to the range of services offered.

What is less clear from the limited literature is what was meant
at that time by information, advice and counselling. In *Youth and
Community Work in the 1970's* the authors state: 'In speaking of counselling we do not mean advising' (HMSO 1969: para. 248). Further

on: 'Counselling is a skill demanding certain knowledge, qualities, training, and practice and is helped through the developing relationship between counsellor and client' (HMSO 1969: para. 253). However they recognize that there were few counsellors in either schools or the Youth Service, although they felt there was a strong case for appointing them (HMSO 1969: para. 255).

In a research report *Advisory and Counselling Services for Young People* Tyler (1978) acknowledges that the term 'counselling' has a 'wide range of meanings' and states that the one most frequently and appropriately used is the 'developmental' model. Linked with this is an emphasis on young people taking responsibility for their decisions. She continues:

> Counselling often overlaps with advice where reaching the right decision is seen to have overriding importance. It overlaps with guidance where the immaturity of the young person is so great that more directive help has to be given, and with psychotherapy where change in established attitudes or patterns of behaviour are needed to avoid mental breakdown, drug-addiction or anti-social behaviour of a serious nature.
>
> (Tyler 1978: ch. 8, para. 9)

She later adds that although counselling is useful in 'conjunction with other forms of help', on its own it is less effective, because of the need for the recipient to be active, motivated and appreciative of the potential benefits. This is an important point. Workers in the field of counselling and information are aware of the difficulties of young people in knowing exactly what services they need. In fact they often require a combination of all three: counselling, information and advice. Services reflect a response to the perceived needs of young people, which leads to the great diversity in service provision. The Tyler report advocates that, rather than developing a specific model, what appears to be essential is 'a sensitive perception of the needs of an area, flexibility in attempting to meet those needs as they change, and realism concerning the type of help which can be given within the resources available' (Tyler 1978: ch. 8, para. 9).

The report also identifies the different philosophical backgrounds that inform these different strands of service. The professional counselling services developing from health-based services tend to use a psychoanalytic model of the personality; and their psychoanalytically trained staff are often from a social or health work background. Counselling services that have formed from within the community tend to be staffed by volunteers, and use a developmental

model similar to that found in the school and career guidance tradition. Their approach is person-centred and based on Carl Rogers's
theory of personality, and therefore very much part of the humanistic tradition.

Broad-based services offering a variety of help are mostly derived
from youth and community work. According to that perspective,
they advocate autonomy and empowerment, and also use a person-
centred model. Along with the social work influence, the emphasis
is on life skills, personal and social education and practical help on
issues such as homelessness. Tyler also lists the specialist services
such as medical, accommodation, drug use and alcoholism, and
minority groups. Their orientation varies and includes a range of
psychoanalytic, humanistic, cognitive and behavioural approaches.
These services use both professional staff and trained volunteers.
Thus, even as early as 1978, we can see core differences between
services that have developed from varying traditions.

The needs of young people have also been identified by the World
Health Organization (WHO), in an attempt to raise European awareness of the emerging services and achieve a more informed response to young people. In its *Summary Report* published in 1978
the WHO stated: 'Youth advisory services should be accepted as an
essential part of overall mental services structure' (WHO 1978: 1).
It saw youth advisory services playing a major role in the network
of community services, able to respond quickly to the changing
needs and demands of young people:

> Youth advisory services characterised by such features as
> anonymity, easy accessibility and central location within the
> community could and did respond rapidly to changing needs
> and demands. However, government at the national and local
> levels often had difficulty in responding quickly to such
> changes, but could sometimes be stimulated by initiatives in
> the non-statutory field. The element of risk-taking which was
> essential in innovatory service should be recognised and taken
> into account when financing such services . . .
>
> (WHO 1978: 2)

Finance is discussed again later in the paper, emphasizing the importance of making funds available even in times of financial restraint, to ensure that contemporary needs of young people can be
met quickly and effectively. The need to work in collaboration with
other agencies is reiterated, so that information and other services
are co-ordinated at both local and national level. Four recommendations are made in the report, acknowledging the need to:

a) Co-ordinate the collection, documentation and dissemination of information about young people, their needs and the youth advisory service available to them;
b) Facilitate the exchange of experience in the field;
c) Provide advice to youth advisory services on professional standards;
d) Provide advice on the selection, training and support of staff for youth advisory services.

(WHO 1978: 2)

The National Association of Young People's Counselling and Advisory Services (NAYPCAS) was founded in January 1975. It was originally part of the National Youth Bureau (NYB) which favoured the growth of youth counselling, but it later separated from this parent organization. Previously NAYPCAS had existed in its own right, but with no paid staff, and at this time the British Association for Counselling (BAC) was its parent body. A break occurred with the BAC as a result of two basic differences in attitudes to counselling. NAYPCAS believed that: first, counselling should be carried out primarily by volunteers in the voluntary sector, and second, that counselling should be seen as part of a multi-dimensional approach of services offered to young people. Youth agencies have always favoured other services – such as information, advocacy and advice – being offered alongside counselling. At a later stage the differences between the two organizations were not so obvious, as BAC itself moved towards a more eclectic membership. However NAYPCAS remained separate partly because of funding, and partly because of the development role inherent in the organization. This is clear from the three aims that were identified at its formation:

1. to be a pressure group;
2. to be a national clearing house for information and training;
3. to be a lobby to get more money for existing agencies.

The organization's membership was made up of paid and voluntary staff from local youth counselling and advisory services, who catered for the needs of young people aged 16 to 25. Funded by the Department of Education and Science, it worked in close contact with, and from the same premises as, the National Youth Bureau. One of its main characteristics was the close links that were developed between itself and its members who were carrying out the work. Unlike BAC, NAYPCAS did not have the resources to develop codes of practice. However, it was able to link BAC ethics to the youth counselling agencies and bring very diverse and disparate services together. At

the time of its inception, the number of individual centres offering
information, advice and counselling had grown, and NAYPCAS itself had 70 corporate and 50 individual members.

By 1984 the numbers of services involved with NAYPCAS had
risen, and included 60 counselling and advisory services and 85
generalist youth work projects, which offered counselling and advice as part of their work with young people. Most of these agencies
were situated in London and the south of England, where greater
affluence enabled more resources to be made available to develop
this work. The NAYPCAS *Policy Document* (1984) advocated the need
for urgent expansion to other parts of England, Scotland, Wales and
Northern Ireland.

It also stated that the main value of youth counselling and advisory work 'lies in its contribution to the personal development and
education of young·people. Its main aim is to foster and develop
personal autonomy' (NAYPCAS 1984: 2). The terms 'youth counselling' and 'advisory work' are defined in the policy as referring to
a 'variety of helping interventions' and responses to young people
in their concerns or difficulties. Key interventions include:

informing – which denotes sharing information;
befriending – which denotes offering practical and emotional
    support;
advising – which denotes recommending action on the basis
    of assessed information;
counselling – which denotes work aimed at promoting self-
    exploration, self-understanding and self-directed action.
                                        (NAYPCAS 1984: 2)

In particular, the document strongly advocates the need for the
provision of suitable secure funding in order to continue and ex-
pend existing provision. It draws on the Thompson report *Experience
and Participation* (1982), which states that an 'assured place' should
be given to provision in local areas of information, advice and counselling. In the Thompson report three ways were identified in which
the Youth Service tried to meet the needs of young people. The
third referred directly to counselling:

Over the past 10–15 years especially, a number of centres have
come into existence specialising in youth counselling on a drop-
in basis, or by phone or letter. These may be funded by the
LEAs, by large voluntary organisations or by small local bodies,
and may use full-time, part-time and voluntary workers. As
we might expect, many of these centres report great difficulty

in funding, owing to the withdrawal or uncertainty of financial support. At the same time most agencies report steadily increasing usage.

(Thompson 1982: para. 5.26)

Thus both the Thompson report and NAYPCAS policy document recognize the state of most agencies at that time as being 'small scale, poorly funded and insecure' (NAYPCAS 1984: 4). This is just as true today, despite the fact that the need for counselling is increasing rather than decreasing.

YOUTH COUNSELLING IN THE LAST TEN YEARS

Over a ten-month period from 1987 to 1988 Her Majesty's Inspectors (HMI) carried out a survey of youth counselling services in 25 local authorities. The Thompson report on the Youth Service had called for 'an assured place' to be given to youth counselling. The HMI survey was able to find some areas of good practice, but the report did not indicate that the situation had improved overall since Thompson. The inspectorate visited 85 specialist youth counselling and information agencies, detached and outreach projects and youth centres. They also sent questionnaires to find out about both policy and provision of counselling in the Youth Service.

They acknowledged the broadness of definition that the word 'counselling' has in youth work, ranging from 'informal, personal help to individual young people' to weekly counselling sessions 'by appointment' (HMI 1989: 3). In summary, they concluded that the range of support and counselling provided to young people fell into five categories:

1 one to one youth work;
2 specialist information and advice work through an agency;
3 informal counselling in a youth work setting by a trained counsellor;
4 formal counselling by selected and trained volunteers;
5 psychotherapeutic counselling by professionally trained counsellors.

Distinctions in these approaches were made in an appendix. From this it becomes clear that categories 1 to 3 are seen as the province of the youth worker, whether trained for the task or otherwise. Formal and psychotherapeutic counselling (categories 4 and 5) required 'greater expectations and demands of both client and counsellor' (HMI 1989: 30). This is because of the contracts, boundaries and commitments that are made between both parties: confidentiality and attendance times, for example, are negotiated as part of this process. The report recognizes the importance of supervision for counsellors working formally. It also points out that levels of training required need to be higher for those working at the psychotherapeutic level.

The diversity of approach and type of service offered is also highlighted in this report. So too is the cost-effectiveness, despite the inherent difficulties most agencies appear to have with funding. It recognizes that many agencies began outside the maintained youth service, originally raising funds from numerous sources such as Urban Aid, district councils, the Manpower Services Commission's Community Programme, Social Services and, regrettably less often, the Youth Service. As much of this funding has dried up, some response has come from local authorities. However it was recognized that the majority of agencies faces considerable financial difficulties. As well as calling for more secure funding for counselling agencies, the report recommends more resources for NAYPCAS to fulfil its development role.

The HMI report makes apparent the uneven distribution of services, the majority being in the south and west with a small number in the north and east. The largest number was situated in London, where the services had a greater percentage of paid, part- or full-time workers, often professionally qualified.

Some research published in 1983 by Anita Sawyer parallels the earlier work carried out by Tyler (1978), although Sawyer restricted her study to the London area. It has similarities with the HMI report (1988). Once more we see the Marriage Guidance tradition represented by Off the Record in Finchley. It began as a result of Marriage Guidance counsellors going into local schools, and eventually led to a youth section of Marriage Guidance in the area.

The psychotherapeutic tradition is represented by the Tavistock Clinic in Hampstead and the Brent Consultation Centre. Both rely on professionally trained therapists offering services in line with the recommendations of the World Health Organization report:

> Their work in the early detection and assessment of psychosocial factors contributing to mental vulnerability and in resolving that frequent adjustment problems of young people was regarded as a major endeavour in the field of primary prevention.
>
> (WHO 1978: 2)

The input from both Social Services and youth work is reflected in The Upstairs Project which combined drop-in services with formal appointments, and a considerable amount of outreach work on the street, pubs and cafés.

Sawyer (1983) also describes 'street agencies', which are similar to Tyler's (1978) 'generalist agencies', offering counselling, advice and information in a specific area. She gives the Soho Project and New Horizon as examples.

The last category identified included specialist agencies such as Rape Crisis, Gay Switchboard and Gay Teenage Group, the Brook Advisory Clinics (pregnancy and contraception), and the Piccadilly Advice Centre (housing), which all offered specific services for identified groups.

RECENT DEVELOPMENTS

Towards the end of 1989 the National Youth Bureau (NYB) had been identified by the Department of Education and Science (DES) as the most appropriate source of service and support for a new initiative of local youth bureaux for 14 to 25-year-olds. The first stage in the process of setting up these bureaux was to consult with young people, and those who worked for them, to discuss the type of provision that was thought to be most appropriate. It is worth noting that a wide range of participants were represented from all parts of the country, including young people, workers from existing projects, professionals, principal youth officers and policy makers.

The result was the publication of *The Local Bureaux Initiative: A Consultation Report* (NYB 1990). It is a key document that brings together many of the points that previous research and reports had already made. There was some debate on the inclusion of counselling in the bureaux. The conclusion was that it would depend on the location of the various pilot schemes: 'It was agreed that if there was no appropriate counselling agency in close proximity to the bureau, counselling should be included as a function of its work' (NYB 1990: 9).

Counselling skills were seen as a necessity for bureau staff, who would offer an integrated approach to information, advice and counselling (NYB 1990: 19). However the stigma attached to counselling was a recurring theme (NYB 1990: 24) and a low-key image was suggested (NYB 1990: 24). It was therefore recommended that counselling should be replaced by the word 'guidance' (NYB 1990: 27). In many ways this is the same theme reflected as in schools, where fears are often voiced that counselling, as opposed to guidance, is outside normal work with young people. To what extent this reflects young people's fears, and to what extent it reflects the fears of people who work with young people, is a matter for speculation. One thing is clear: whatever the arguments, the cost involved in setting up such projects is very large.

It might be helpful at this point to look at the provision that has developed in The Netherlands. Youth advice centres are found throughout the country, situated in every province, and funded by the Dutch Ministry of Culture (90 per cent) and by the provincial government (10 per cent). Known as JACs, they are places for young people to go who are experiencing problems at home, in school, at work or with the police. Funds are provided to pay the salaries and ancillary expenses of workers who are usually in their early twenties to thirties and already have a profession. In addition there are students on placement from local schools of social work. Until 1992 they were also reliant on volunteers, but a case was made to the government that such important work should be valued, so now all workers are salaried.

Some of the work by the JACs is carried out in specifically designated buildings and some within the community by outreach work. Advocacy and mediation are offered by these services. Pressure is exerted on the government through a national network of JACs to change law and social policy for the greater benefit of young people. Publicity is given high priority to ensure young people know about the centres. This is done through the schools, medical facilities and in the local paper. For example, every week an article is featured on 'how to make a benefit claim' or 'how to find a room'. Good working relationships are established with local specialist agencies such as the FEHGG, which offers counselling to young people from 13 to 23. Ongoing counselling is not within the province of the JACs, as they prefer to concentrate their resources on more direct and political involvement. In recent years funding has become an issue and the way forward for them is to make alliances with other bodies (i.e. in Utrecht, the ambulance and day care service) to put pressure on the government and province to allocate more funds. Hence they are able to argue from a much stronger position than is possible in Britain as we shall see.

In many ways the youth bureaux system is similar to the Dutch model. Perhaps one reason that formal counselling is not part of the British structure is because of the difficulty in finding suitable young people to train to the levels required, as well as the financial implications of providing such training. Some organizations seek to provide basic counselling training for volunteers, often based on the 'Egan model' (see Chapter 2). This, however, is more likely to occur where centres have better funding or are part of the Youth and Community Service.

Much of the political work that the JACs are involved with was also carried out by NAYPCAS, but in 1990 the DES decided to channel its funding through one single, high profile and comprehensive National Youth Agency (NYA). In establishing the NYA, the DES had in effect fully merged the Council for Education and Training in Youth and Community Work (CETYCW) and the NYB, which were already part of the same administrative unit. The NYA received Government funding to support both the voluntary sector and specialist counselling and advice bodies. This left the membership organizations of NAYPCAS and the National Council for Voluntary Youth Services (NCVYS) with the alternative of either dissolving themselves or competing for a much-reduced grant under a separate scheme. Faced with this decision the NAYPCAS Executive Committee attempted to get separate funding. It achieved this for three years, moved premises, and in May 1992 changed its name to Youth Access. Now a much smaller organization than the original NAYPCAS, Youth Access is made up of an institutional membership which (in the words of its mission statement):

> BELIEVES that all young people have the right to make informed decisions through ACCESS to Information, Advice and Counselling and PROMOTES the development of high quality Information, Advice and Counselling through Consultation and Training.

What will happen when the funding runs out remains to be seen. Hopefully this organization, which is so important in the field of young people's counselling, being the only one providing a national network, will attract the funding required to continue its work. However in the present climate, with major resources already channelled into the NYA, the outlook is far from optimistic.

In this chapter we have documented the growth of counselling for young people in the post-war years as well as the development of the concept of adolescence. The societal changes that have taken place in the last half-century and the pace of that change have added to the pressures and difficulties that have always been inherent in this life stage. Having reviewed the historical development of counselling services to young people, in the next chapter we will consider the situation at the present time.

· TWO ·

Counselling for young people

In this chapter we discuss theoretical models for working with young people and describe some of the contexts in which this work takes place. It is important at this stage to make a distinction between the use of counselling skills and formal counselling. Many professionals and volunteers who work with young people use counselling skills in their work. For example, nowadays teachers, youth workers and social workers learn effective ways of working one-to-one with their client groups and will acquire the skills of active listening as part of their training. Many workers attend counselling courses or in-service training where such skills can be learned or further developed. These skills are then used informally to improve communication and facilitate the delivery of the service involved. Formal counselling is the contracted relationship between counsellor and client where the two parties meet at an agreed time and place for the sole purpose of the counselling interview.

FOUR THEORETICAL MODELS FOR WORK WITH YOUNG PEOPLE

The person-centred approach

The person-centred model is widely used in work with young people in Britain. This approach to counselling, based on the work of Carl Rogers, lends itself particularly well to work with the young, who, through their experience of the core conditions of empathy, unconditional positive regard and congruence created by the person-centred counsellor, are able to mature and develop.

A person-centred practitioner understands distress and disturbance in terms of a conflict between the real self, usually referred to in person-centred theory as the organismic self, and the self-concept. The latter is the constructed, internalized, sense of the self based on the expectations of significant others and the denials and adjustments the individual makes to gain the approval and positive regard that are essential for emotional well-being.

For example someone brought up in a household where she was told that jealousy is bad, with the implication that 'good people are never jealous', is faced with a dilemma if she experiences jealousy. She may deny the emotion: 'I never feel jealous, I am not feeling this', or if she acknowledges the feeling will perceive herself as bad. In another home where jealousy is accepted as a natural feeling inevitably experienced on occasions this dilemma would not occur. Persistent denial of feelings eventually results in a lack of sense of self. Persistent self-vilification leads to a sense of worthlessness and low self-image.

Difficulties such as these described above are established in early life but exacerbated in adolescence through the introduction and influence of the peer group. In addition, adults who generally feel inhibited and constrained from passing judgements on the attitudes, behaviour, demeanour and way of being of other adults, exercise no such restraint with regard to young people. Every aspect of their lives is open to scrutiny in both the private and public sphere and they are constantly subject to censure and criticism.

It is through the medium of the core conditions, empathy, congruence and unconditional positive regard that counsellors, working in a person-centred way, facilitate the work of young people. *Empathy* requires counsellors to attempt to see the world through the client's eyes, to temporarily suspend their own perception and, through active listening and attending to the client, to understand what it means to be the client in their particular life situation. In order to do this counsellors must be willing to engage on the emotional level. They must be willing to recognize the client's feeling by recognizing and acknowledging in themselves the emotion being described or felt, while simultaneously focusing on the client and being aware of the separateness between them. The process is as follows: 'My client is feeling sadness, I know how I have felt in sadness, this can help me to understand and to stay with my client in this sadness.'

In counselling young people, intense, raw emotions can be encountered. This can make it difficult to maintain empathy and stay in touch on an emotional level. In addition, young people frequently describe their interactions with adults such as their parents and their teachers as difficult and problematic. Many counsellors are nearer in age and attitude to these adults than to their young clients and there is therefore a risk of losing empathy and identifying with the adult participants in the conflicts described. This is the nature of the challenge presented by work with young people: is the counsellor willing and able to be alongside the young person as they explore the confusion, the rebellion and the failure?

Unconditional positive regard – the intrinsic valuing of the client without imposing conditions of worth – is of particular importance when working with young people whose sense of self-worth is often low. The experience of being with someone providing this core condition is healing in itself and will enable young people to begin to challenge their self-concepts and pay attention to the promptings of their organismic selves.

Holding clients in unconditional positive regard does not mean that counsellors will not challenge or confront. To the contrary, the process of separating people from their behaviour – of intrinsically valuing clients – enables counsellors to make confrontations and the client to tolerate and make use of them. This is in contrast to most challenges to young people which take place within a very different and less sustaining framework.

Congruence, the last of the core conditions, requires counsellors to be as real and authentic as possible within the counselling relationship. Essentially congruence means meeting a client person-to-person. A young person, experiencing congruence on the part of the counsellor, meets a professional person who is not hiding behind a facade or a role but who is responding in a real way, as one human being to another. There is equality within such a relationship that will be both welcome, and empowering, to that young person. Through the experience of congruence, the young person will be able to learn to trust and perhaps most importantly will be shown a model of a way of being that involves listening to feelings and valuing them.

Congruence is distinct from self-disclosure, which is an inappropriate sharing of the counsellor's personal life. This is burdensome to all clients and particularly difficult for young people, who already have enough of their own life to cope with. The value of congruence is in keeping the relationship between the counsellor and the young person alive and vital. It allows for ongoing evaluation of the relationship and the work, which would include acknowledgement of what is going wrong and apologies where appropriate.

An illustration of the person-centred approach to counselling young people is the case study of a young man who we shall call James.

James is nineteen years old and was referred to a young people's counselling service by Victim Support after he had been the victim of a serious assault. He is a good-looking, articulate young man from an Irish background who welcomed the opportunity of some one-to-one attention. He was very open and in the course of the first four sessions told the counsellor a great deal about what transpired to be a very difficult life.

James was the outcome of his mother's incestuous relationship with her uncle and was her first child. She was understandably very ambivalent towards this child, who she saw as both her ally against the world and the personification of her sin and shame. James had a long history of sexual abuse, being the victim of his stepfather and his own father. After being taken into care he was assaulted sexually by a teacher at a residential school. He then had to give evidence at the subsequent trial of this man.

In his early teens James had had some involvement in drugs and at sixteen he had worked on the streets as a rent boy. Lately his life was somewhat improved as he was living in a housing project, had a job in a clothing shop and was in a stable relationship with a man in his mid-twenties who James felt really cared for him. However, in the housing project he again became the victim, this time of bullying and ridicule, related to his quite effeminate presentation. Things became increasingly difficult and after refusing to hand over money, James was attacked and beaten.

Two things about James struck the counsellor very strongly. First was the way that James would be very watchful and alert for her responses to him. He would then attempt to accommodate her. Second, James had no sense of outrage or even self-pity about the way he had been treated. Another significant factor was that James did not, in the early stages of the work, keep to his contract. He would arrive late or miss sessions but when confronted with this was extremely apologetic, appeasing and full of excuses.

Over the weeks, the counsellor worked hard at creating an atmosphere in which James felt respected, valued and understood. She attempted to gain his trust by being as consistent and real as possible. The work was slow but gradually James began to get in touch with his feelings of sadness, loss and eventually anger and outrage. Instead of always reacting and accommodating he began to explore what he wanted, thought and felt.

At his instigation they examined strategies for sticking up for himself and challenging others who offended him. This culminated in his successfully confronting someone at work who was attempting to make him the butt of yet another joke. James sense of self-worth began to grow and he gradually developed stronger boundaries with other people. James was in counselling for almost 15 months and by the end he was a challenging and demanding client, very different from the accommodating person he had been at the start. He had at last begun to value himself and though he had many problems, he was no longer a victim of life.

Egan's three-stage model

Many young people's counselling services who would see themselves as philosophically aligned to the person-centred approach, but who are constrained by time and financial considerations, use Egan's three-stage model, which is essentially a problem-focused way of working. This model breaks down the counselling process into three stages.

In the first stage, the young people are encouraged to explore their current situation and identify problematic areas. Working from this new-found clarity and awareness, in stage two the clients set goals and objectives and explores what life might be like if some of the options available to them were taken up. In stage three, the clients are encouraged to go on to develop action plans and strategies for the accomplishment of the goals they have set themselves in stage two.

This way of working, being problem-focused, lends itself particularly well to short-term contracts. However it could be argued that such a structured approach is not person-centred. The following case study illustrates the approach.

Anne was a student at a sixth-form college. She felt completely swamped by the conflicting demands of her A level course and her social and family life. In stage one of the work Anne identified that she felt as though she was forever juggling the various demands on her time. As a consequence she was failing in her academic work and not enjoying the free time she managed to arrange for herself. She also acknowledged that she was resenting the demands made on her by her invalid mother and her father, who had passed a good deal of the responsibility for the housework, cooking and shopping to Anne.

In the second stage of the work Anne explored what she really wanted and found that her priority was to gain the results she needed to ensure university entrance on a languages degree. She also wanted to sort out the domestic arrangements so as to regain her previously good relationship with her parents. Lastly, she acknowledged the importance of her having some free time to herself to socialize with her friends and play some tennis, which she greatly enjoyed.

In the third stage Anne worked out strategies for approaching her father to discuss the domestic arrangements. She decided to suggest that he employed a cleaner, which was financially feasible. She examined her study skills and came up with academic work timetables which she shared with her father so that he would respect them. She also programmed in free time, including the whole of Sunday, when her father could cook, to ensure she had a proper break from all her responsibilities.

Anne continued coming for a few sessions to monitor her progress with the goals she had set herself. Success soon became evident as her grades picked up and she felt more in charge of her life. Her counselling had taken place over eight sessions.

The existential approach to counselling

The existential approach to counselling is particularly pertinent to work with young people. As Emmy Van Deurzen-Smith states in her introduction to *Existential Counselling in Practice*:

> The type of counselling proposed involves assisting people to come to terms with the dilemmas of living. Issues are addressed in moral terms rather than in terms of sickness and health. The frame of reference is philosophical rather than medical, social or psychological. The assumption is that people need to find ways of making sense of life before they can make sense of their problems and of themselves.
>
> (Van Deurzen-Smith 1988: vii)

This approach, based on the writings of European existential philosophers, does not seek to solve problems which are inherent to human life, but to gain insight into the many paradoxes that are unavoidable as a result of living. As with all therapeutic orientations there is a set of implicit basic assumptions:

1 It assumes young people are capable of making well-informed choices about their own life as well as their attitude to it.
2 It assumes that it is both desirable and essential for young people to have a consistent frame of reference to make sense of their life and experience.
3 It assumes counselling is a process of clarifying and reflecting to discover the meaning in one's life, often through questioning of one's own basic assumptions and of confronting the paradoxes and dilemmas of human living.
4 It assumes young people create meaning in their world by their own attitudes to life and thus reap what they sow.
5 It assumes there is no ultimate chaos or ultimate order, but meaning and order can be created in spite of seeming chaos and absurdity.
6 It assumes human nature is intrinsically flexible so that whatever the given factors of a person's life, the *response* to those circumstances is not determined and can therefore be chosen.
7 It assumes that the given factors are limitations on human life within the given boundaries of birth and death. These limitations are based on physical and biological principles, such as ageing and sickness, which limit us to some degree to what we can or cannot do, though not how we respond.

Existential counselling is an exploration of the young person's being-in-the-world and how they relate to and understand that world. Young people, as we saw in Chapter 1, are moving through a period of transition from childhood to adulthood, and dependency to autonomy. This is a time when adolescents question social and moral values and look for an identity of their own. Thus an approach which relies on a questioning attitude to the way one lives one's life, as well as an acceptance of the need to explore one's relationship to the world, is very appropriate to this life stage. The existential counsellor will help the young people explore their 'worlds', of which there are four, although to a certain extent these all overlap. They are the natural world, the public world, the private world and the ideal world.

The *natural* world is the basic dimension of human existence that everyone inhabits. To understand a client's relationship with the natural world is to explore how they relate to the physical world, and will include their body image, their bodily reaction to internal and external stimuli, physical fitness, and attitudes to food, sex and nature. Thus a sense of the client's being-in-the-world is gained, as well as an insight into the extent to which they find it essentially alien or friendly.

The *public* world focuses on the young person's relation to their race, class, culture, language, family, reference group, work environment and attitudes to authority and law. This is the social world where power is always an issue. People can choose to be dominant, submissive or withdrawn in their response to encounters with others, but people often get stuck in one of these modes of functioning. It is in this arena that adolescents in particular have difficulties and may experience a tension between egoism and altruism.

The *private* world is characterized by the relationship one has with oneself and one's ability to be intimate with others. It is concerned with the individual's identity and includes how a person evaluates their previous experiences. If individuals are not comfortable with their own identity it will affect how they relate in the other worlds. Adolescence is a time for young people to sort out their thoughts, feelings, ideas and aspirations. However, society tends to place greater importance on functioning in the public world, leaving the young person more concerned with relating to others than relating to themselves. Yet the two are interlinked: people who are not comfortable in their private world will often lack the strength and flexibility of character to relate effectively in *any* world, as the case study on p. 35 illustrates.

Finally, the *ideal* world is the dimension of ideas and beliefs associated with the other three worlds, and it also points beyond them. Therefore an individual's spiritual, religious or non-religious philosophy of life is encompassed both in the present and beyond. Some people are unaware of this dimension, of something greater than themselves, which can lift them above everyday struggles. This is a person's internal truth and is pivotal to the way that an individual makes sense of the world. External truths, which are not internalized, give structure but do not give meaning on a deeper level, and therefore are more likely to disintegrate if challenged by crisis.

The counselling process is an examination of all these interconnected worlds. Young people may have more difficulties in some worlds rather than others, although all will be affected and therefore cannot be ignored. The following case studies are an exploration of the worlds of three clients, to show how they overlap and interrelate. The case studies also give an opportunity to explore the four ultimate concerns of existence and the conflicts which arise from them. These are the existential issues of death, isolation, mean-inglessness and freedom. However because adolescence is such a turbulent time these fundamental concerns are often just below the surface of what may appear to be quite superficial worries.

Death

Death is a primary source of anxiety, according to existential coun-selling, and the tension between the awareness of the inevitability of death and the wish to continue to be is a core conflict in life. There is considerable evidence that children become aware of death and of their own mortality at an early age (Yalom 1931). Realizing their life will end causes them great anxiety. Children will deny the inevitability of their own death by believing in personal specialness, omnipotence and invulnerability or by hoping that some external force will deliver them from their fate. In adolescence, young people have to confront the question of their personal finiteness and move away from the childhood stage of denial.

Young people sometimes become obsessed with the idea of death, in particular the denial of death, through activities which are inher-ently dangerous such as riding motorbikes or cars at high speed, or participating in high-risk sports, sometimes not adhering to safety procedures. This dicing with death and defying its inevitability is all part of the omnipotence and invulnerability syndrome, which can be shattered when a person close to you dies. However any death can bring about an ontological crisis as it forces us to face our own mortality.

Tina was an 18-year-old student studying to go to college. When she presented for counselling the counsellor was struck firstly by her dress which was exclusively black. She said she was bored with her studies and no longer felt she wanted to continue. Her speech had a monotonous tone and Tina ap-peared to be relatively depressed. The only thing to which she became animated were her 'Gothic' clothes and her outings to gigs where she was able to meet other Gothics. In the ensuing weeks the counsellor learned quite a lot about Gothic culture which is concerned with death. It subsequently emerged that the young woman had encountered death twice in the past year. Once as a result of the death of her baby sister which had affected her family, particularly her mother. Tina herself denied having much to grieve about as the baby was so young. The second death was a friend and Tina was more concerned with giving support to other friends than looking at the impact this had on herself.

Death is the boundary to life and facing one's own death usually leads people to assess their life and the meaning it may or may not have. Other people's death, particularly people one is close to, also confronts one with finiteness and often creates a need to find personal meaning and assessment of one's own life to that point. Tina was affected by both deaths and created her own way of dealing with it by her involvement in Gothic culture. As the counselling progressed she began to make more sense of her feelings of boredom. They were an indication of the sense of meaninglessness that accompanies loss of security in the world. Thus it is often through confrontation with death that people find a new perspective on life. Death shifts one away from the preoccupations of life and can be a catalyst to a more meaningful existence.

Meaning

As we saw earlier, meaning plays a focal part in this form of counselling. Meaning helps us to relieve the anxiety that comes from facing a world without an ordained and comforting structure. Meaning gives us a framework to the way we live our life and enables us to develop values that in turn synergistically augment our sense of meaning. In our present culture, through striving, creating and achieving, people find their meaning. However this emphasis is a fairly recent development and some cultures would even question the concept of 'purpose in life' (Yalom 1931: 467), and would exchange the concept of 'doing' for 'being'. In this way, life becomes a journey, rather than a goal-orientated endeavour which emphasizes the past and present as a preparation for the future. A goal-orientated purpose will eventually invite the question of what is the future, and what happens when goals have been achieved?

Adolescence is a threshold, a time of being neither a child or adult. Young people are about to embark on a new journey and have to come to terms with who they are and how they want to be in the world. Pressure comes from all sides to achieve, succeed, accept and follow society's expectations, which are based on a 'doing' or goal-orientated model of life's purpose. There appears to be little opportunity for reflection except within this given framework. Yet for a great many young people it is this very basic level of meaning which often underlies their concerns about the future.

Some therapeutic orientations, like the Egan model, offer a problem-solving approach which fits well with our cultural ethos but perhaps fails to address the underlying question of meaning and finiteness. As we saw in the previous case study, confrontation with death led to meaninglessness for Tina, but she was able to create her own unique way of dealing with the resultant anxiety by immersing herself in Gothic culture. By entering her private world, the counsellor shared her need to make sense of the events of her recent past. She engaged with her, relating authentically within the context of her world. As Yalom states:

> . . . when it comes to meaninglessness, the effective therapist must help patients to look *away* from the question: to embrace the solution of engagement rather than to plunge in and through the problem of meaninglessness.
>
> (Yalom 1931: 483)

Isolation

There are three types of isolation. *Interpersonal* is generally experienced as loneliness and feeling apart from other individuals, whereas in *intrapersonal* unacceptable parts of oneself are partitioned off and there is a sense of distrusting one's own thoughts and feelings. *Existential* isolation is described by Yalom as 'an unbridgeable gulf between oneself and any other being' and a 'separation from the world' (Yalom 1931: 355). A dream brought by an 18-year-old client demonstrates this type of existential isolation.

> I am sitting on a chairlift clad in ski gear. It seems as if the world is covered in snow, the world is frozen, dead. I look around me to see if I can see anyone, but no one seems to be around. I then notice figures coming towards me, on the chairlift as I go up the mountain and they come down. To my horror they are not just dead but merely skeletons and I realize I am the only person left alive in the world.

This sense of being ultimately alone is another cause of existential anxiety and is unavoidable to human existence. It is normal, not pathological. As we grow up and separate, we move towards independence and self-reliance and we are forced to confront the world's loneliness, mercilessness and nothingness. This experience of intense isolation is described as 'dread'. Because interpersonal and existential isolation are inextricably linked, it is important to separate oneself from the former in order to encounter the 'dread'. When aloneness is faced a person is able to engage more deeply and meaningfully with themselves and with others. Interpersonal relationships may moderate the feelings of existential isolation but they will not eliminate them. There is no solution to isolation as it is a part of existence. Thus the existential conflict lies in the tension between our awareness of our isolation and our wish for contact. It was only when the young woman who had the dream began to face the fear of isolation, experience the dread, that she was able to manage the anxiety the dream left her with.

Freedom and responsibility

In the existential sense, freedom refers to the absence of external structure. As the individual does not enter a well-structured universe, they find themselves in fact responsible for, and author of their own world, life, choices and action. A key existential dynamic is the clash between our confrontation with groundlessness and our wish for meaning and structure. Young people on their journey to adulthood begin to realize the new freedoms that age bestows and the responsibilities that accompany them. In youth, the conflict between freedom and responsibility is played out many times. Sometimes it may emerge as a fear of leaving home and going to college, sometimes as leaving college and taking up employment. It can be both exhilarating and fearful to realize that one is the author of one's experience and that any encounter with the world or with people means an acceptance of the part we play ourselves. Young people can fear the freedom and the responsibility. It is so much easier to blame, parents, teachers, society and the world at large.

> Mark was a 16-year-old pupil who was having difficulty in class. He was unable to relate to the other members because, he said, they had different interests to him. He did not even want to try to be interested in their pursuits, as he did not approve of them. He was interested in his subjects but he felt they were not taught well enough and the other pupils 'mucked around' and made it impossible for him to learn or do his work on time. Homework was also a problem as the teachers did not explain things clearly enough and at home there was too much noise to work. Mark was a Christian though he despised the people who went to his church as he thought they only went to look good. His parents, he felt, were okay, although he believed his mother was rather two-faced: in the

home overly critical but outside a paragon of virtue. Each
attempt that the counsellor made to get Mark to see if he had
some part to play in any of his life experience was sidestepped
by another grievance. However he kept on coming and very
slowly he made a little progress in taking some responsibility.

Mark initially had little desire to take charge of his life, he preferred
to be the victim of circumstance. It was only as the relationship
developed with the counsellor that he could begin to see that he
had choices and that those choices would determine the way he
experienced his world. Much of his rigidity was focused on the
external structure he imposed upon himself with his Christian faith.
His ideal world was based on 'shoulds' and 'oughts' rather than
internal truths. These rigid structures give a sense of security but
can lead to a very restrictive life, as in this case. With a loosening
of the rigidity Mark found he did not fall apart and eventually was
able to function better in the public world.

Existential counselling is about enabling the young person to
experience choice within the confines of the 'givens' of existence.
Young people today, perhaps more than ever, feel constrained by
social expectations which may not be made explicit, but are implicitly conveyed culturally by our education system in which young
people spend, at the very least, 11 years. Time to reflect or just to
'be' is not encouraged by our society. When young people experience anxiety, the existential counsellor sees this as an indication of
awareness of their freedom to make choices and take responsibility
for them, which in itself creates anxiety. Anxiety, therefore plays a
fundamental role in life and is basic to existence. It is often only
through experiencing anxiety that we recognize our fundamental
concerns: how we are choosing to live our life and whether it is
'authentic', that is, true to our innermost being. To live authentically is to become increasingly capable of following the direction of
our own conscience. It is in direct contrast to feeling a victim of
one's life or fate, or of feelings of imposed duty and expectations
from without. Existential counselling encourages the young person
to go in the direction conscience dictates with the realization that
this will inevitably bring responsibility towards oneself and towards
others, and will include the experience of both success and defeat.

Using a psychodynamic perspective with young people

Psychodynamic theory is based on the work of Freud and contributed to by post-Freudian, neo-Freudian, and the Object-Relations

schools of thought. Inevitably there is great diversity within this framework which cannot be covered here. Rather, we will present three aspects of the theory which we think are particularly relevant to work with young people.

An understanding of the term 'psychodynamic' gives us an insight into the the practice of the counsellor using this approach with the client. 'Psychodynamic' is made up of two words: 'Psyche', which means mind, emotions, and the spirit of the self; and 'dynamic', which implies the relation these parts have to each other and to people and objects outside of the self. Some of this activity is conscious and available to the person, or accessible from a preconscious state, and some is unconscious, although on occasions available through dreams, fantasies and 'Freudian slips'. One of the aims of psychodynamic work is to make this unconscious activity conscious, to enable the client to balance the conflicting demands of his own inner processes, outer relationships and external reality. As Jacobs states:

> The primary purpose in psychodynamic counselling is to help clients to make sense of current situations; of feelings and thoughts evoked by those situations; of memories associated with present experience, some of which spring readily to mind, others of which may rise to consciousness as the counselling develops; and of the images that appear in fantasies and dreams. From this wealth of material, all of which is important to the psychodynamic counsellor, counselling attempts to form a picture, representing not just the way in which the client relates, or wishes to relate to others, but also the way the client relates to her- or himself.
>
> (Jacobs 1988: 10)

The psychodynamic approach is based on a developmental theory of personality, with childhood being particularly significant. Personal history is therefore an important factor for the counsellor, and is used to help the client understand their behaviour in the present. It could be argued that when working with young people conflicts which arose in childhood can be more accessible, although also more frightening as the young person has not yet developed such effective defences against emotional trauma. Ellen Noonan's book *Counselling Young People* (1983) is an excellent introduction to using psychodynamic counselling with young people.

The three aspects of this approach that we will focus on are transference and counter-transference, maintenance of the frame, and containment.

Transference and counter-transference

The relationship between client and counsellor is the crucial element in the counselling alliance. However, psychodynamic work,
more than other forms of counselling, brings to the forefront the
interaction between the two parties. The immediacy of what is
experienced in the relationship can reflect the way the client responds to others outside of the counselling room. Transference is
described as:

> ... the client is transferring or placing qualities of someone
> else (usually someone from the past) onto the counsellor and
> then responding to her as if she were that person. His behaviour
> is thus inappropriate, an illusion. The unreality of the trans-
> ference arises from the fact that a past relationship is actually
> being recreated in the present – not just being remembered or
> retold – and this results in some perceptual and emotional
> distortion of the counsellor and the relationship. Generally it
> is an unconscious process, so the client is not aware of what
> is happening or what feelings and qualities are being revived.
>   (Noonan 1983: 86)

The person-centred approach tries to provide positive experiences
for clients through empathy, congruence and unconditional positive regard. The psychodynamic counsellor, although empathic, is
not only concerned with any positive transference feelings but also
with any failures that might reflect what a person has experienced,
in the belief that by allowing the client to relive the pain of the past,
they may work through these painful feelings in the present. This
is why the 'frame' holds so much significance in psychodynamic
counselling, as it holds the client through these uncomfortable times.
In the same way, breaks and endings have particular significance,
for they enable the client to experience loss or a sense of being let
down, within the context of counselling, thereby giving the client
an opportunity to work through early frustrations and losses in the
present.

Counter-transference refers firstly to the feelings evoked in the
counsellor by the client, perhaps complementing the client's transference as well as the counsellor's own personal transference of
unconscious material from the past. It is sometimes difficult to dis-
tinguish between these two, which is why supervision is particularly important in this context. The counsellor's own transference,
whether it be negative or positive, might impede the process of
counselling whereas thoughts and feelings experienced from the

complementary counter-transference can enhance the process, as it may give the counsellor an insight into the way the client can make others feel or, indeed, what the client feels.

Perhaps one of the difficulties in working explicitly with transference with young people is that, for a great many of them, short-term counselling is the norm, often for four to six weeks. Explicit use of transference heightens the interaction between client and counsellor which makes it uncomfortable for very short-term work. This does not mean that transference is not used implicitly by a psychodynamic counsellor to inform their understanding of the process of the relationship. The fact that the counsellor is very likely to be closer to the age of the client's parent than the age of the client gives a heightened intensity to the parental transference that needs to be especially carefully and sensitively handled with young people.

A simple example of working with transference issues is demonstrated in the following piece of dialogue:

Client: I don't know why I am here, I'm wasting everyone's time.
Counsellor: You seem to be concerned that you are wasting my time.
Client: My Dad says I'm a complete waste of time, I haven't got a job. I'm messy in the house and he doesn't like my friends.
Counsellor: How do you feel about that?
Client: I wish he would stop getting at me and judging me all the time.
Counsellor: Are you afraid I am judging you or that I will get at you and see you as a waste of time?

Maintenance of the frame

In this context we are using the word 'frame' to describe the contractual agreement between client and counsellor, as well as the professional boundaries that the psychodynamic counsellor brings to the work. These boundaries, the elements of the agreed contract that creates the framework and the maintenance of this frame, both confronts the client with the issues that need to be worked on and provides the security for that work to take place. In this respect counsellors from other orientations have a great deal to learn from the psychodynamic approach because much bad practice in counselling results from poor boundaries and frame violations.

The contractual issues that have most relevance to young people

are those related to keeping to agreed times, coming for the agreed
number of sessions etc. Issues of control are of real significance to
the young, who may well experience the contract and the counsellor
as rigid and controlling, losing sight of the fact that they have freely
agreed to come. This could be an example of transference, wherein
the client experiences and responds to the counsellor in a way that
is inappropriate to the counsellor's actions or behaviour. It is as if
the client's experience of another signiflcant person in their life
becomes attached to the counsellor, however inaccurately, and they
respond accordingly. This gives the counsellor a valuable insight
into how the client might also relate to others in their world and,
if skilfully picked up by the counsellor, can be extremely productive.

Another reason young people may have for keeping to the contract is that counselling touches on deep and painful issues and
strong resistance may therefore be encountered. This can be mani-
fested in missing sessions or coming late, and needs to be explored
and understood with the client. The counsellor would be well
advised to reflect upon the content of the previous session and to
consider the pace of the work. For example, a young male client
was in counselling because of some confusion about his sexuality.
He was a reliable person who usually came on time to his sessions.
One week he did not attend but the following week came as usual
and explained that he had missed his bus and had not been able to
find a working public phone. He carried on coming regularly and
then after several weeks he missed again. This time he explained
very apologetically that he had just forgotten. Again he returned to
his pattern of regular and punctual attendance. When he missed for
the third time his counsellor went back through her notes and
made the connection that on each of the sessions prior to the missed
appointments her client had been alluding to transsexualism and
his terror of his feelings about himself and his desire to be female.
Here was the key to the missed sessions.

Adolescence is a permanently shifting sand, and psychodynamic
counsellors, through their attention to boundaries and the process
of counselling, can provide the young person with a safe place in
which to explore difficult and painful issues. The separateness and
relative anonymity adopted by the counsellor both facilitates the
transference and provides the client with the space in which to do
the work.

Containment

Within the psychodynamic framework the relationship between the
counsellor and client mirrors key relationships in the client's life,

such as mother and child; father and child; siblings; and significant others. Just as in the early years of life the mother or primary carer is the 'psychological container' for the child, so in the first stages of counselling the counsellor is available to 'contain' the client. Through the transference relationship the client may experience and recognize the inevitable frustrations inherent in these early relationships and the ensuing distress and anxiety. Recognizing and experiencing these early conflicts leads to exploration, and hopefully understanding, of how these manifest themselves in later relationships, including the relationship with the counsellor. The counsellor contains these feelings and helps to make sense of them in order that the client can develop and mature emotionally and move towards autonomy. This is a developmental task that, in adolescence, may be being replayed for the first time. The relationship between a successful conclusion of the individuation process and the conflicts of adolescence is crucial. A successful counselling intervention at this stage may prevent these conflicts from continually being played out in later life. Endings are an important part of this process and the psychodynamic counsellor will pay particular attention to these for two reasons. First, the ending of the therapeutic relationship may bring into focus other losses and endings for the client, and these may not have been acknowledged or resolved at the time. The psychodynamic counsellor will wish to work with the ending of this relationship in a way that acknowledges its importance and allows expressions of all the feelings involved. Second, there will be a concern to review the progress of the work, allowing space to express both positive and negative feelings towards the counsellor and the counselling.

YOUTH ORGANIZATIONS

In the previous chapter we saw that youth counselling, outside of a formal education setting, has its roots in a variety of organizations and has led to a broad perspective in services offered. Many of these services have funding from different sources. However, increasingly, the Youth and Community Services who are traditionally providers of leisure and social activities for young people have seen themselves as a provider of social education. In this role issues such as race, gender, class, sexuality, and citizenship, among others, are addressed by youth workers when working with young people informally. Counselling and group work skills have become a prerequisite of a good youth worker. A national shift has taken place, from a service based in youth clubs to one which includes project and outreach work with young people in the community. This has led to the individual needs of young people being recognized as diverse and not always in the province of the youth worker. Young people themselves are also making their needs known, leading to a greater acknowledgement of the need for services designed specifically for them.

Since the 1989 Children Act a wider interest has been shown in the social development of young people who are vulnerable or at risk. More recognition is given to the need for the support of local authority services and this has led to a number of inter-agency ventures. For example, in Hertfordshire the Youth and Community Service has developed a number of collaborative projects, which have enabled different groups of young people to benefit socially, emotionally and behaviourally. These have been set up between the Youth Service and the Hertfordshire Constabulary, Social Services, the District Health Authorities, Education Welfare, schools and the Probation Service. Such collaboration has led to the provision of opportunities for teenage mothers, the homeless, those at risk of offending, young unemployed and those whose health is at risk. Waltham Forest, like Hertfordshire, has also been involved in this type of inter-agency work and has similarly given high priority to young people's participation in the setting up of projects.

Youth counselling in the community is diverse, not just in the type of centres that have emerged, the services offered, and the staffing available, but in the funding and support such services can elicit. It appears that one of the underlying reasons for this diversity is a result of the various types of response to the needs of young people that occur in different regions.

In many agencies, counselling is part of their ethos usually offered in an informal way where the main service function is offering information, advice or advocacy. Most informal counselling occurs as a result of someone seeking information or advice, where it becomes important to enable the person to clarify issues and feelings while providing the necessary 'holding' or support required. This could then lead to further help through a referral to another agency or to formal counselling if the issue is of an emotional rather than a practical nature. Some agencies dislike this rather rigid demarcation, feeling that when working with young people all their needs can and should be responded to by the worker concerned. This is certainly the ideal within the advice work field. However, as with any age range, some require a more specialist resource provided by someone trained in more than basic counselling skills. This is what we refer to as 'formal' counselling in this book.

To understand further what is offered by different agencies and how they work in practice we describe three models that incorporate many of the diversities mentioned above. How these agencies translate their aims into practice is unique to each.

Signpost – predominantly a counselling agency

Signpost was conceived in 1973 through the interest of a local doctor and a few volunteers. It was six years before it offered any real service. Like many agencies of its time, it arose out of a professional's perception of the needs of young people rather than being user led. Regular funding was eventually gained from Youth and Community and Social Services, and it also achieved charitable status. After a number of changes of address it has settled just off the High Street in Watford. At the present time, its funding is reasonably secure compared to many agencies. Hertfordshire Youth and Community Service is committed to developing information and counselling, which has led to extra part-time hours being made available for workers. In addition a new post of co-ordinator has been created to expand the service into other areas of South-west Herts, as part of a comprehensive county approach.

Signpost has always been predominantly a counselling service for young people and/or their parents, although at one earlier point in its history a more informal approach was adopted as a result of being situated right in the town centre. This is now not so and counselling is mainly by appointment, Monday to Friday from 9.00 a.m. to 9.00 p.m. with a drop-in facility on a Saturday morning. Apart from the co-ordinator there are four part-time staff each working 14 hours a week. This includes an office and information worker who manages the induction of volunteers and co-ordinates the office administration and two outreach workers. The latter liaise with other agencies, visit schools, and deal with publicity, with one being responsible for work with Asian young women and the other for setting up a free pregnancy-testing service. In addition, a development worker with the homeless manages the 'Crashpad' scheme to provide emergency accommodation for young homeless people, and also advocates on their behalf. Another important role of this worker is to co-ordinate a team of volunteers to interview young homeless people, find them accommodation and put pressure on statutory agencies to provide more facilities. So it can be seen that between them the team has a wide variety of responsibilities and roles that reflect the complexities of young people's needs.

Volunteer counsellors are recruited from the large range of

counselling diploma courses in the area. At present there are 30 counsellors working at Signpost and another six working in satellite provision in Bushey, Hemel, and Berkhampstead. One consequence of recruiting from courses that attract mature people means that the majority of counsellors are between 30 to 40 with some being older. Local courses were predominantly psychodynamic in orientation, and this is reflected within the agency although less now than in former years, as more courses offer an integrative approach. Present counsellors offer person-centred, systemic or existential approaches. All counsellors are in group supervision on a fortnightly basis, with individual supervision provided when required by the counsellors. Supervision is offered voluntarily by outside agencies, such as the Child and Family Clinic, and counsellors at the local Further Education College, as well as volunteers from the agency itself who have previously worked as counsellors.

Information workers (approximately 18 in number) staff the phone and deal with information queries, mostly on the telephone. They are younger, usually in their twenties. However despite attempts to develop the youth enquiry side, Signpost is still seen as having a mainly counselling focus even though other services are provided.

It is clear that there is a need for this type of provision, as is seen in young people's use of the service. During the past year the counselling provision expanded and the take-up doubled. Signpost workers are now committed to providing a quality service where no young person need wait for more than four days before being seen for ongoing counselling. Anyone arriving at Signpost during office hours will be seen immediately and if appropriate, referred to a counsellor. The size and type of building restricts the possibilities for running an enquiry service, although, as we go on to describe, these are successful elsewhere. It will be interesting to see if in the future, more areas of the building can be made available by the Youth and Community Service for the development of a more comprehensive information service.

Centre 33 – formal counselling and information

Centre 33 started in 1970 as a joint venture of both Cambridge City and County Council in conjunction with Cambridge Health Authority. Situated in a quiet street, yet close to the city centre, Centre 33 has enjoyed the benefits of regular and consistent funding since its inception.

Both counselling and information are offered by the service and the two are described as working alongside one another as a 'seamless garment'. Volunteers are recruited to work either as part of the information service or as part of the counselling service. Centre 33 staff are keen to make no hierarchical difference between the two sides of the service, rather they see them as complementary. At the present time there are two full-time members of staff, one to co-ordinate the counselling the other the information service. A third member of staff on a four-fifths post develops outreach work in schools and youth clubs. They are also provided with 25 hours of paid administrative support, something rare in such services.

Counselling is by appointment, but anyone can drop in when the centre is open, which is on Monday, Tuesday and Wednesday from 10 a.m. to 1 p.m., 2 p.m. to 5 p.m., and 6 p.m. to 9 p.m. On Thursday it is closed all day, but on Friday and Saturday morning it is open from 10 a.m. to 1 p.m. A pregnancy testing and counselling service is offered on Saturday. Counselling may be one-off, short-term (approximately six weeks), or long-term (a year or more).

Counselling is offered on person-centred principles, and counsellors are recruited from certificate or diploma courses. Centre 33 offers its own training, which consists of 20 weeks, three hours a week of theory and practice. This enables an equal opportunities approach to recruiting counsellors, from age ranges not normally accepted on to courses, and people from groups who are under-represented among the counsellors, such as black and Asian. All counsellors are expected to have had some therapy or counselling. Information workers also have a 12-week training on subjects which include accessing information, the benefit system, and listening skills.

Group work is offered in schools, and therapeutic group work has recently been instigated as a result of an extension of the premises. Centre 33 has two satellite services, one in a GP surgery, the other in a youth centre. It has a comprehensive supervision system, offering fortnightly individual supervision with outside paid supervisors. Information workers are also provided with a good support system.

Off the Record – information, advice and counselling

Off the Record describes itself as an information, advice and counselling service for young people in Avon. It came into being as a result of interest from two agencies, the British Association of Youth Clubs and Marriage Guidance, who provided the premises and a reception service until 1975. Originally the service was more counselling-orientated until Marriage Guidance withdrew in 1975. Then, new premises were sought, and Off the Record became increasingly in-terested in developing an information and advice service to meet the varying needs of young people. The service was set up in 1965 and became an independent charity with its own management committee in 1971. In the 10 years up to 1981 the number of users was approximately 500 per year. Since the mid-1980s these numbers have tripled as a result of new premises and a full-time worker. Based in Bristol, Off the Record consists of a shopfront that contains a waiting area and information area, and two floors which provide two counselling rooms, a group room and an office.

Funding is provided from Avon Youth Service and a number of other small grants and donations. However funding is a major concern for Off the Record, which has had its grant aid cut over the previous few years. It is at present attempting to expand its funding base so as to be less dependent on the Youth Service which, nationally, is subject to large cuts in expenditure and staffing.

At the present time there are two full-time workers and one part-time worker who manage the service and provide training, as well as professional and administrative back-up for the team of volunteers. Originally all volunteers were recruited as 'counsellors' although they worked in information, advice and offered informal counselling. One of the repercussions of the 1990 budget cut was to reduce the amount of training that the service could provide to potential volunteers. Now, each volunteer has to commit herself to two years of work with the agency for an average of nine hours a week in order to be considered for training. After selection, reception workers attend a training course of about 12 hours followed by an observation period, and work is begun in the offlce during this time. Welfare rights training is available for a six-week period for all workers, as well as a basic counselling skills course.

Counsellors are required to do a course of 40 hours duration spread over five months, which is an introduction to the Egan model of counselling. This is followed by six months of supervised work and a further review of the Egan model. Some volunteer counsellors will then go on to fund themselves for a diploma course. Supervision is provided every month in a group for two hours, and support is also provided by pairs of volunteers using a co-counselling model. As with Centre 33, one consequence of offering in-house training is the recruitment of a much broader group of people.

The distinction between information and counselling is purposely not so marked as in the two previous services because it is felt that young people are not as likely as adults to make a clear demarcation between these different functions. Counselling is described in the Off the Record Procedures Manual as 'a way of relating and responding to people as individuals so they are helped to explore their feelings and reach a clearer understanding before taking any decisions and acting'. This can be done in the context of information or one-to-one counselling. Advice may be offered after the presentation of information to enable young people to see the way forward. However although decisions are made by the young person, action 'may be taken by, with or for them'.

The service is open on Mondays to Fridays between 11.30 a.m. to 3.30 p.m.; Tuesday evening from 6 p.m. to 8 p.m., and on Saturday morning from 10 a.m. to 12 noon. The service is open to young people and people concerned with their welfare. Although no age group is specified, 70 per cent of clients are between the ages of 8 and 30.

Off the Record's greatest difficulty for the future is to secure regular and broader-based funding. As one of the pioneering services in the field it regularly faces closure each financial year, and the paid workers have set up their redundancy provision in case money is not forthcoming. Recently they have had to lose one part-time worker and reduce the amount of counsellor training programmes.

COUNSELLING IN EDUCATIONAL SETTINGS

We have seen in Chapter 1 that the word 'counselling' is used in schools in a very wide context, covering advice giving, careers guidance, and disciplinary meetings. Although much was written in the seventies about counselling in schools, in recent years there has been little at all. It is, therefore, interesting to note that in *Pupil Welfare and Counselling*, published in 1990, the definition of counselling proposed was:

> In counselling, one individual, the counsellor, works with an-
> other, the client, to clarify the nature of some problem expe-
> rienced or presented by the client, and to explore possible
> solutions. Counselling can also take place in a group but the
> essential characteristics remain, namely that it is problem ori-
> entated, and that it involves the interrelated stages of clarify-
> ing the nature of the problem and exploring possible solutions.
>   (Galloway 1990: 4)

In this definition, counselling is seen very much in terms of being problem-solving and solution-focused, and in contrast to the definitions in youth work settings, the 'emotional' element is missing. In other words it is nearer a cognitive or behavioural approach. The next sentence is further illuminating: 'An essential issue in our

definition of counselling is that many, perhaps the majority of interviews in school are held at the request of the teachers, not of
pupils or their parents' (Galloway 1990: 4).

What is stated is that very often the pupil is not 'choosing' to be
counselled, rather the teacher perceives the problem and a counselling interview may result. This point is discussed in more detail later
in the book where Galloway suggests that although all interviews
could be seen as counselling, it is really only those where 'the problem is generally regarded as the principal focus' (Galloway 1990:
66) that *are* counselling. However most counsellors would not see
the problem as their principal focus, nor would they regard an
interview not chosen by the client as a starting point for counselling
unless the client's agreement had been negotiated. We feel this is
an important distinction to make in order to clarify what is, and
what is not counselling in the terms of this book. An enormous
amount of useful work is carried out by teachers in schools that is
more accurately defined as mediation, negotiation, advocacy, guidance and advice, rather than 'counselling'.

Following the industrial action taken by teachers for increased
pay, the Burnham pay scales were abolished and the government
introduced conditions of service requiring teachers to take part in
pastoral arrangements. As we have seen there appears to be a greater
emphasis within schools on developing a more integrated pastoral
system, which has led to less employment of counsellors as such
although greater acknowledgement of the usefulness of counselling
skills. Very few schools employ counsellors to work on a one-to-
one basis with pupils, and teachers themselves, however committed
to the idea of counselling, do not have the time to offer more than
informal counselling within a tutorial session or lunch hour. At
present there is little evidence that schools who have opted out of
local authority management are choosing to provide formal counselling for their pupils within the school.

Among the few who are employing counsellors, there appears to
be two distinct systems of ethics and practice in use which have
parallels to those outlined in Chapter 1. Tim Bond's article 'Ethical
issues in counselling in education' (Bond 1992, 20 (1): 51–63) takes
the debate further. The first is the *integrated* model, similar to Law's
'system orientation'. The second is the *differentiated* model, similar
to the 'open orientation'.

The *integrated* model sees the counsellor as having the same relationship to the school as other members of staff, and counselling
is offered in the context of being compatible to the goals of both the
student and the institution. In the case of a comprehensive school

this will be the learning opportunities offered. As Bond states: 'In this view it follows that the counsellor's primary responsibility is to promote the well-being of the organisation through work with clients and contributing to its policy decisions' (Bond 1992: 52). This is done primarily through the pastoral system. It has shifted the emphasis in the school from only valuing the dissemination of learning and knowledge, to seeing pupils as whole people who need skills and support as well as knowledge. If the ethos of schools promotes 'respect for the integrity of the individual learner, and impartiality in the relationship between teacher and students', then Bond (1992: 53) feels it would bring the same values, of respect and impartiality, to education as those stated by the British Association for Counselling (1992) and the British Psychological Society (1985). Perhaps this is somewhat optimistic. Daws states, having surveyed recent trends in education designed to make it more child-centred and more concerned with pupil welfare as a whole, that he felt that child-centred theories were unlikely to be a threat to schools in the foreseeable future. Even at their most popular they impinged little on the school curriculum and where they did, they came under heavy criticism.

The *differentiated* model distinguishes the relationship between counsellors and other staff members in the school, because the counsellor is seen to have a primary ethical responsibility to the client rather than the organization. An individual client's autonomy is safeguarded and standards of practice are comparable to those working in Further and Higher Education. Naturally these two models will lead to differences in ethical issues. These will be discussed in Chapters 3 and 4. It is significant to note here that Bond (1992) sees the necessity for the client to both choose to take up counselling and choose the material to work on as being implicit in both models. Although the two models are significantly different in other ways, the context within which each is used could be an important variation. Bond suggests the integrated model would be preferential in educational settings that work with younger and/or more 'at risk' clients, whereas the differentiated model perhaps lends itself to a more mature clientele.

When talking to counsellors working in schools, whether from an integrated or differentiated perspective, there appears to be a greater emphasis on problem-solving models of counselling than is found outside of education. Some examples of these are:

• Problem-solving systems (Priestley *et al.* 1978) cover social skills as well as problem-solving techniques;

- The DOSIE system (Nelson-Jones 1987) provides a framework to structure problem-focused work in five stages. The first is to describe and identify the problem, the second is to state the problem operationally, the third is to build skills followed by setting goals and negotiating interventions, then finally exiting by consolidating self-help skills. In the initial stage, the working alliance is built on the usual person-centred core conditions;
- The three-stage model of Egan (1975) is referred to earlier in this chapter;
- Rational emotive therapy is based on the work of Albert Ellis (1977). Here clients are taught to think 'rationally' rather than holding on to irrational or illogical beliefs about themselves and the world.

Counsellors in schools are also more likely to use a wide range of methods which, as we have seen, may include cognitive and behavioural theories as well as the affective models that are more common in youth counselling agencies. In this way, perhaps a little optimistically, counselling is seen to be tailor-made to the client.

THE WORK OF THE EDUCATIONAL WELFARE OFFICERS

Educational welfare officers, usually referred to as EWOs, are staff employed by local education authorities to carry out the statutory responsibility of the authority and ensure that children of school age are receiving education appropriate to them. Once known as truancy officers, the name was changed either to educational welfare officers, or in some authorities, educational social workers in an effort to shift the emphasis away from their policing role to more accurately reflect their supportive role. As well as their responsibility for truants and school refusers, they often administer small grants available to support children of school age, for example, maintenance awards and travel grants. Despite this work being notoriously badly paid, it seems to attract able individuals from a variety of backgrounds, many of whom are skilled at balancing their statutory responsibilities to enforce school attendance with the need to establish real working relationships with the young people and families with whom they work.

In many authorities, EWOs are going into schools and homes to work on an individual basis with young people who are having difficulty in going to school or remaining there for the school day. Before any serious sanctions are taken against these young people, EWOs use counselling skills, or on some occasions, formal counselling to help the young people to understand and face up to their difficulties. This is always done with the clear agenda of getting them back into education or supporting them in remaining there. This agenda will always limit the counselling work to some degree. In addition, as with all local authority employees, the extent to which they can offer confidentiality is limited, particularly with regard to the disclosure of abuse. Nevertheless they do some sterling work, without much appreciation. The supervision offered to them, particularly for their counselling work, varies enormously from authority to authority and is at best patchy.

SPECIAL PROVISION

Despite the best efforts of educationalists to ensure that as many young people as possible are educated in mainstream schools, there remains a minority of young people who, because of the extent of their physical or mental disability or their behavioural or emotional disturbance or social circumstances, are unable to cope with mainstream schooling. The nature of special provision is various. Some schools are staffed and equipped to provide for the needs of young people with severe physical disability. Units can be set up to cope with young people with challenging behaviour, and home tuition may be provided. However the extent and the quality of the provision varies enormously from authority to authority and because it is essentially a marginal activity, it is particularly subject to cuts in times of economic retrenchment.

Because of the nature of the work and the client groups involved in this special provision, the institutions tend to be much smaller than mainstream schools and the staff-to-pupil ratio much lower. This allows for more one-to-one contact. A little less pressurized by numbers and the demands of the National Curriculum, they are able to develop a creative, flexible approach to education that is at root, student-centred and in which the use of counselling skills and formal counselling is a recognized part of the approach.

A good example of this is the North Herts Secondary Centre. This unit takes up to 30 young people from years 10 and 11 (14 to 16 years of age) from secondary schools in its catchment area, which is the whole of North Hertfordshire. Young people referred to the centre would include those who are disaffected with, or under-achieving, in mainstream schools; students with particularly challenging behaviour (including some who have been excluded from other schools); and school refusers and students who feel unable to cope with large institutions. Others who may be referred are those who are experiencing conflict either in school or at home, students who have been bullied and those who would benefit from a smaller and more supporting, secure environment with a greater level of adult contact.

The ethos of the centre is informed by person-centred thinking. Of the seven members of teaching staff, (five full-time and two part-time), two hold diplomas in counselling and one studied counselling as a substantial component of another course. Counselling skills are used by all members of staff and contracts of behaviour are negotiated with the students. Where disputes occur between students, or where there is a history of difficulties between them, they are encouraged to have a dialogue until difficulties are resolved. Interpersonal skills, such as assertiveness, are part of the curriculum and there is considerable emphasis on building the self-esteem of the students.

Formal counselling takes place when it is requested by the students themselves, or it may be offered to students manifesting distress. It is generally undertaken by the head of the centre, who is one of the staff members holding a diploma in counselling. It may be either a one-off session or a series of sessions, depending on the circumstances and needs. Inevitably there will be some distortion of the counselling process as a result of its delivery by someone who has other relationships with, and responsibilities towards, the young clients. Nevertheless, the head of the centre felt that the ethos of the centre was such that this role change could be managed by both counsellor and clients and that productive work could take place.

As county council employees, the contracts of confidentiality offered by the staff at the centre are limited. There is also no consultative supervisor for the counselling work, although the majority of time at the weekly meetings of the staff group is given over to discussion of one-to-one work with students, thus acting as an informal peer supervision group. Previously an educational psychologist could be called upon for supervision, but as that person had left the area it was no longer available. Currently, particularly difficult cases can be discussed with a senior EWO, who is very supportive to the work of the centre, but this cannot realistically be described as counselling supervision.

THE DUDLEY COUNSELLING SERVICE

Since the late seventies, the Dudley Metropolitan Borough Education Department has been providing a counselling service for the young people in its schools. It was originally part of the educational psychology department but then became a free-standing service. The counselling service is staffed by fully trained professional counsellors, whose numbers in this time of recession had been reduced to six, but are now once again on the increase. It is greatly to Dudley's credit that it has maintained and supported this apparently unique service. The counsellors are employed on teachers' conditions of service and paid on mainscale teachers' salaries.

Counsellors are assigned three or four secondary schools, with whom they will form close working relationships on a peripatetic basis. Relationships with staff in the schools are generally very positive. Over the years the service has been running, the schools have come to understand the service and its function. Although the main focus of the work has been at the secondary age range, some support has been offered to the primary sector, which has been well received. Referrals generally come through the schools' pastoral system although occasionally students can self-refer. Sometimes parents might also request that their son or daughter receive counselling. Unfortunately, however desirable it might be, it is not feasible to operate an open door policy because of time constraints.

Once a referral has been accepted, an initial interview will be arranged. This first session is for assessment purposes; if the referral proves to be appropriate and the young person is agreeable a contract will be made. For legal reasons relating to visitors in school, the parents' permission must be sought if the student is going to see the counsellor. The counsellor we interviewed said that in most cases this was quite manageable, when sensitively handled. Nevertheless, on some occasions young people were unwilling to enter into the contract if their parents were to be informed. Some parents, for a variety of reasons, found the idea unacceptable. Once they agreed, however, the contract was very much with the young person and no further contact with the parents would take place without the freely given consent of the young person.

Because of time constraints, counsellors are in the individual schools for a minimum of a morning and afternoon each week. Ideally clients are seen once a week, although this is not always possible. Sometimes it is fortnightly to allow greater numbers of students access to the system. The counsellor we interviewed generally offered blocks of three or four sessions to clients because he felt that this would be both manageable and acceptable to young people unused to the idea of counselling. At the end of each set of sessions clients would review the work and see if they wanted to continue. Although some of the work was relatively short-term, some students may engage in long-term work and one or two came consistently throughout their school career.

The theoretical bias of the service has tended to be humanistic although some staff have come from a psychodynamic background. Dudley has been generous in its support of ongoing training and has thus ensured that the counsellors have been able to keep up to date and broaden their skills base. Supervision, for an hour and a half a week, has been peer-based, although support has been available from the senior counsellor. However it could be argued that such important work would benefit from external consultative rather than managerial supervision.

Counsellors working in schools with people as young as 11 or occasionally younger need to be flexible in their approach. Some of the work is skills-based. For example, students often require help to develop strategies for coping with academic demands, or they may have difficulty in expressing their emotions – particularly anger – in ways that are acceptable within the school environment. The mission statement for the service states that they wish 'To provide a confidential Counselling Service to pupils with social, emotional or behavioural problems to help them function effectively at school' and the wide ranges of referrals seem to reflect this. It is only to be hoped that Dudley continues with this bold and highly effective initiative which all parties seem to agree has served its schools well for so many years.

In this chapter we have explored four models of counselling theory and their application to working with young people. We have also considered a variety of settings in which this work takes place. We have attempted to give a flavour of the diversity of services available, and of the strengths and weaknesses inherent in them.

· THREE ·

The practice of
counselling for young people

In this chapter, we will be exploring the way in which some issues, common to all counselling, relate specifically to work with young people.

CONTRACT SETTING

One of the life skills we need to learn as we grow up is that of negotiating a contract. Living or working with other people, raising children and many of life's most important functions involve working out with the other person how we are going to go about the task in hand. This involves clarifying our expectations and responsibilities, keeping to the agreements made, while trusting the other person to do the same. The process of negotiation within relationships needs to be ongoing if they are to be kept alive and vital. Unfortunately our society gives children little say in and power over the course of their lives, but nevertheless we expect young people to have this skill without providing them with the opportunity to learn it.

It is for this reason that the process of setting the counselling contract with a young person is both extremely important but also fraught with difficulty. For some it may be the first time they have been given the power and responsibility that is implicit in the making of a contract. It is therefore important that the counsellor makes no assumptions about tacit agreement but takes the time and trouble to set the contract clearly, while ensuring that the young person is an equal and willing partner. This will set the tone for the rest of the work.

The counselling can usually start by checking with the young person how they have arrived in counselling. This is important because not everyone has the same understanding of the word 'counselling' and other professionals or parents may well have sent the young person to be 'counselled' out of what they perceive to be difficult or challenging behaviour. Thus counselling may well be perceived by the young person concerned as part of a policing process. A counselling relationship built on such a misconception is doomed to failure from the outset.

Another possibility is that the young person may feel that counselling is a 'stay of execution'. An example of this was a sixth-form student who was found to be smoking marijuana. She was initially threatened with expulsion. This would have been catastrophic for her as she was a very bright and highly motivated student who had gained a place at a much sought-after university. In order to be allowed to finish her course, she had to agree to a package of measures and sanctions. One was that she had to be 'counselled' about her 'drug habit'. Of course she agreed. Had she been told she had to run around the town each day with a bucket on her head she would doubtless have agreed to that too. Doubtless too her motivation would have been similarly minimal.

When a client feels they have been 'sent', they cannot freely enter into the counselling contract. This does not make counselling impossible, but it is vital to give the young person time to understand both what is on offer and what is expected of them as clients in this unique relationship. They can then decide whether this is what they want. Paradoxically, the freer young people are to say no to counselling, without risking censure or criticism from the counsellor, the more likely they are to stay and to use the time available to them positively and creatively.

In private practice there is another important issue in contract setting with young people, relating to who pays for the sessions. The old adage 'he who pays the piper calls the tune' comes to mind. When an adult decides to go to a counsellor in private practice the financial transaction that takes place between the two is both important and significant. Paying represents commitment to the work. A service is being purchased by the client from the counsellor. No favours are being imparted. The transaction is straightforward and lends itself to the creation of an equal working relationship between the two.

With young people, the existence of a third party may muddy the waters. Either the parents or some other institution are likely to be paying for the work. The young person is not being called upon to demonstrate commitment through payment. The other party in the transaction may well feel that they are entitled to some say in the process and outcome of the work, or that they have the right to know what goes on in the sessions. It is essential to clarify these issues with all concerned before the work commences, thereby ensuring both that the young person really wants to enter the counselling relationship and that everyone appreciates that it is the young person who is the client and is entitled to confidentiality.

Young people coming into counselling need to appreciate the extent of the confidentiality that can be offered to them. Those counsellors who are employed by institutions are constrained by their obligations to their employers particularly with regard to the disclosure of abuse. They therefore cannot offer confidentiality to young people in the way that is available to those working with adults. All local authorities have policies and procedures that bind those who work for them, including counsellors. In addition, a counsellor has statutory responsibilities under child protection legislation, which will be discussed in detail later. Suffice it to say at this point that it would not be ethical to offer complete confidentiality when this is not really available.

It would be an understandable reaction for those counsellors, used to a high degree of autonomy and a low degree of institutional accountability, to throw up their hands in horror at this apparent intrusion into their preserve. This, however, would be an over-simplistic response that does not understand the nature of work with this age group. There are procedural and legislative requirements and complexities – and in order to effectively work with young people these need to be recognized and understood. In addition, it is necessary to liaise with other agencies and to create co-operative working links.

Counsellors working with young people are sometimes invited to attend case conferences. These meetings provide the opportunity for all the professionals working with a young person, or in some cases with the family, to get together and discuss the situation to ensure that they are working co-operatively and that the client or clients are getting the best service possible. Sometimes they are contracted after a crisis has arisen or when a major decision, for instance, whether or not to take children into care, needs to be made.

While some counsellors would not even consider accepting such an invitation, on the grounds that it would violate the boundaries of the counselling relationship, others think differently and would attend in order to offer support to the young person who is the client. Of those who would attend, some would do so if the client was to be present, some would attend only in a supporting role and would not speak, while others would take a full and active part.

Although we assume the good faith of those who would choose to attend there are nevertheless important questions that need to be asked. First we need to think about whether or not a counsellor would attend a meeting of this nature about an adult client. If the answer is no, then we must consider how and why the work with a young person is being viewed differently. Is this understandable desire to protect and advocate on behalf of the client really appropriate to a counselling relationship, and how might it affect the dynamics within that relationship? Finally we need to consider if it will be possible to return to the former footing after the meeting and, if not, whether the client has lost something that was uniquely supportive.

This is an example of a broader dilemma faced by counsellors working with young people. On some occasions this client group must be treated differently, and on others this is less clear. It is a delicate balancing act. There are no clear guidelines and counsellors need to constantly monitor their own practice, raising these conflicts and dilemmas for discussion.

TIME AND COMMITMENT

Making appointments and maintaining a commitment to counselling is more of an issue with young people than other client groups. One way of helping young people to take the first step towards counselling is through an informal drop-in service. Young people are less able, in general, to wait for appointments, particularly if there are long waiting lists. A drop-in service bypasses this difficulty. They can turn up on the day and see a counsellor, get a feel of what counselling is about and then have the opportunity to commit to ongoing counselling if they feel the need. A drop-in provides a taste of what counselling will be, and allows people to be seen quickly in a crisis situation, often preventing a more difficult situation arising. A typical example of this is the young person who walks out after an argument with a parent. They have nowhere to go but feel unable, at that point, to return home. The drop-in gives the young person an opportunity to discuss the situation with a counsellor who allows the expression of all the feelings and then encourages the exploration of the available options. This can facilitate the young person returning home to begin a dialogue with the

parent. Where appropriate, further ongoing support may be negotiated with the counsellor on a weekly basis or a one-off session
may be sufficient. In either case, the young person has had an
opportunity to explore their options, release their feelings and choose
a path most suitable for themselves in the circumstances.

For some young people open-ended contracts can seem daunting,
so many counselling agencies, including those in schools, negotiate
a six-week contract including a review session. In this structure
there is a boundary to work to, which can always be renegotiated.
However, many young people do not turn up consistently for sessions
regardless of how the contract is formulated. This is an important
area for the counsellor to address, as young clients are more likely
than other groups to use absenteeism to express their ambivalence
or fears about counselling.

THE ISSUE OF POWER WITHIN THE COUNSELLING
RELATIONSHIP

To deny the existence of the dynamic of power within any counselling relationship is either naïve or dishonest. Clients are vulnerable, often in a highly charged emotional state, sometimes regressed
and are sharing with the counsellor aspects of their lives in which
they perceive themselves to be failing, having difficulty or feeling
shame. Counsellors, operating in accordance with their individual
philosophies and orientation, are offering empathy, support and
psychological holding but they are not bearing their souls or making themselves vulnerable. Clients are likely to perceive their counsellors as emotionally stable individuals who manage their lives
effectively. This may or may not be true but these differences in
roles and perceptions place the power within the relationship very
firmly in the hands of the counsellor. If we then add to this equation issues of age, race, gender, class, sexual orientation and disability then the complexities become obvious.

Economic and political power is firmly held in this country by
those in the middle years of life. The young and the elderly are not
valued. We have much to learn from Asian cultures, which rejoice
in the wisdom of the old, or from Mediterranean cultures where
children are valued and welcome everywhere. Despite the best efforts
of educators and legislators, generally young people are not taken
seriously. This engenders in many of them a suspicion about older
people whom they correctly perceive as holding more power than
themselves. It is sometimes difficult for them to believe that they

will be listened to and that their opinions, beliefs, perceptions and feelings will be accepted as valid. For many, their experience has been to the contrary.

Counsellors working with the young are often handicapped by the young person's low expectations of any interaction with people from a different age group. This may manifest itself in a surly demeanour and in an unwillingness to engage. It is all too easy to respond in a reactionary and judgemental manner, thus confirming the young person's view. It is only by experiencing the relationship with the counsellor that the young person will learn to trust and open up. For some this will be a slow and laboured process involving a good deal of boundary testing. It is not uncommon for young people to try to shock or challenge their counsellors to the point where they feel they will be rejected. They need to check out if they will be safely held and contained in the work. In other words, the counsellor needs to allow boundaries to be challenged while not allowing them to be destroyed or damaged. Counsellors have to walk the thin line between real acceptance of their clients while avoiding collusion or condescension, both of which will usually be picked up in seconds by the young client.

Black and Asian people are underrepresented in counselling as in all other professions. In all too many cases, young black and Asian people finding their way into counselling are liable to see white counsellors, with no choice being given. This can be problematic with any age group but is particularly so with young people who may, as discussed above, feel alienated from the counselling process. The difficulties inherent in working cross-culturally should never be underestimated particularly with the ever-present spectre of racism looming in the background. There are two crucial and central questions that counsellors need to ask. First, how are young blacks and Asians to find their power and autonomy in the relationships between themselves and their counsellors? Second, how are white counsellors to monitor the way in which they use or misuse their power in the counselling relationship?

Counsellors working cross-culturally have a responsibility to inform and educate themselves about the cultures from which their clients are coming. It is always important to check assumptions, but care needs to be taken that this does not lead to clients becoming burdened with the responsibility of teaching their counsellors about the cultural differences between them. It is not the clients' responsibility to do so.

In areas where counsellors from other cultures are available, services are sometimes faced with the uncomfortable fact that some of their users may be unwilling to see counsellors from their own community. This is particularly so with Asian young women who sometimes experience their culture as too constraining and are afraid that confidentiality will not be maintained. This is a very contentious issue and one that can cause difficulty within an agency. Clients' wishes must be respected but at the same time the credibility of Asian counsellors needs to be supported and their willingness to provide appropriate services to young people from their community affirmed.

When working with the young, counsellors must always be aware that clients coming from minority groups often find themselves in the position of having to straddle two cultures whose values and ways of being are greatly at variance. For example, a woman counsellor was working with a young Asian woman who was having a relationship with a young Asian man from a different religious background from her own, she being Sikh and he Muslim. Although they were 18, both young people knew that their families and their communities would strongly disapprove of this liaison. Her father was already talking about setting up some introductions for an arranged marriage. At a certain point in the work the client began to discuss the possibility of having sex with her boyfriend. Obviously this is always an important decision for any young woman, but in this case it was vital that the counsellor understood the possible ramifications of this course of action which were profoundly different for her than for one of her peers from a white or black British family.

She needed to think carefully about the possibility of her love affair being discovered by her family or community, about the possibility of an unplanned pregnancy and about the possibility of her going ahead with an arranged marriage at a later date having made such a deep emotional commitment. She needed her counsellor to understand her dilemma in a manner that was both respectful and sympathetic to her and her culture.

Racism is always an issue in counselling where one of the two parties comes from the dominant culture and the other from one of the many that are oppressed. It goes without saying that it is the responsibility of all counsellors to be constantly raising their awareness, challenging and inviting challenge on their attitudes and assumptions and using supervision to monitor their practice. In addition, those counsellors working with the young need to be aware of how racism affects young black and Asian people in this country and how their access to power and control over their lives and choices is thereby limited.

It is always difficult to stay with a client in their grief, pain and anger, but when the counsellor is a member of the dominant group and has benefited from the very evil that has caused these feelings, then the task is even greater. When young black people are expressing their feelings about these issues it is all too easy for the counsellor to radiate so much guilt and discomfort that the client stops, and starts caring for the counsellor. Guilt can also make the counsellor unwilling to hear and validate the young client's experience of racism, and the pain, anger and damage that it causes. In this way the counsellor inadvertently uses power to prevent these feelings being shared. If white counsellors are to work with young black people then they must deal with their guilt in a way which does not involve further oppressing clients.

Issue of race, and those of class, gender, sexual orientation, age and disability, in the provision of counselling for the young inevitably raises questions relating to recruitment and training of counsellors working with this age group. We will be discussing later the introduction of NVQs (National Vocational Qualifications) which should go some way to redressing this balance.

THE ABUSE OF CLIENTS

The abuse of clients sexually, emotionally and financially occurs within counselling as it does within all caring professions. If anything, the nature of the counselling interview, generally two people alone in a room, makes clients particularly vulnerable. When the client is young and less powerful the risk is greater still. Most counsellors do not set out to abuse their clients and the provision of good supervision and management greatly reduces the risk of the development of unprofessional relationships. However, a great deal of informal counselling is done without the provision of good supervision or indeed any supervision at all. This is both alarming, inappropriate and potentially dangerous. The intricate emotional dance that is counselling must be properly monitored in order that both counsellor and client are protected and cared for. If institutions want to use workers with counselling skills, they should do so responsibly. This entails providing the support to enable their employees to work safely and effectively.

SUPERVISION

Supervision that is both regular and ongoing has become an essential requirement for counsellors in Britain. As the *Code for Counsellors*

states: 'It is a breach of ethical requirement for counsellors to prac-
tise without regular counselling supervision/consultative support'
(BAC 1992: B.3.1).

The need for good counselling supervision has been acknowledged by young people's counselling agencies both in the voluntary
sector and in county-based counselling services. However it has not
been recognized so clearly in schools. Counsellors need supervision
that is non-managerial and independent. Many counsellor/teachers
have fought to get supervision paid for whereas others have worked
without, or paid for their own. Others working in voluntary agencies
reach a reciprocal arrangement whereby the counsellor gives some
hours to the agency in exchange for outside supervision.

Counselling supervision is considered to be essential for a number
of reasons. First, it provides a system of personal support for the
counsellor, which is particularly important when working with young
people who may be in emotionally, physically or sexually abusing
situations or who have self-mutilated or attempted suicide. Given
the nature of the problems they are working with, the counsellor
can become over-involved, particularly when no one else knows
about the situation. This support enables the counsellor to check
her work in other ways, such as whether she is avoiding painful or
difficult areas. For example, a counsellor was finding it difficult to
acknowledge the suicidal feelings of a young man about to enter
university, who although intelligent and attractive, was in despair.
The counsellor repeatedly avoided the painful and desperate feelings and concentrated exclusively on the positive and on future
possibilities. Supervision enabled her to explore her difficulties in
this area and to disentangle her work with her client from her own
fears about her teenage sons.

Although support is important for all counsellors, the above example illustrates the particular need for this effective back-up when
working with young people. However working with this group can
be particularly anxiety-provoking and worrying. They are at a vulnerable life stage where the risk of suicide or attempted suicide is
high and where difficulties can rapidly become crises. Workers need
help to contain their own anxieties so that they can effectively
contain those of their clients.

Second, a supervisor needs to be able to draw the counsellor's
attention to ethical issues of standards and practice. This may be in
the context of the counsellor's own work or of the agency. The
issue of child protection is particularly significant when working
with the young. This will be dealt with in detail in Chapter 5.

Third, supervision is an arena where the counsellor can continue to learn and reflect on their counselling practice from a wider perspective. This is the case for both individual and group supervision. Individual supervision enables the counsellor to gain further insight from the supervisor, who will ideally have experience of counselling young people and the particular issues unique to this type of client work. Group supervision provides both peer support and insight gained from other members. Tim Bond argues in *Standards of Ethics for Counselling in Action* (1993: 163) that this is a better learning forum because other people's cases often raise issues in one's own practice that would otherwise remain unrecognized. As experienced supervisors working with many groups from young people's counselling services, we would agree with this wholeheartedly. It is particularly true for new counsellors who have not worked with this client group before or are still in training. A great deal of mutual support is generated among supervisees. Issues that are frequently raised are the perennial problem of the lack of commitment of young clients and concerns over the clients' well-being and where the counselling work also relates to a counsellor's own family and personal life.

These three tasks of supervision are often described by the terms *restorative, normative* and *formative*. It is important to get the right balance between the three so that no task predominates to the exclusion of the other two.

Tim Bond (1993: 161) adds a fourth category, that of *perspective*. This deals with an overview of the total counselling work in the context in which it takes place. In a school it would include the relationship with other members of staff and other helping provision such as the tutorial or pastoral system. It would also include relationships with outside agencies, for example, Social Services or a young person's counselling agency. In a counselling agency this would include issues of access, referral to other agencies and relationships with other professional bodies. Most of this would be the job of the agency co-ordinator in conjunction with team members. However these issues of context do inevitably feature in counsellor supervision.

In order for counselling supervision to be effective, a safe environment of trust needs to be established and this is why it is best sought from independent supervisors outside the agency or school. An atmosphere of confidentiality and privacy is then more easily established and maintained and the counsellor will feel able to express anxious feelings and vulnerability in a contained and supportive setting.

Counsellors sometimes need to deal with their frustrations concerning the agency itself. Again this can be done with an independent supervisor. Supervision which is not independent can particularly inhibit the airing of negative feelings which ultimately can be detrimental to the client. Unfortunately, as we have stated, it is difficult in schools to receive any supervision, let alone supervision of an independent nature. In larger agencies dealing with young people this is less problematic, although many rely on volunteer supervisors as much as on volunteer counsellors. This sometimes means that the supervisor does not have particular expertise in working with this age group. However, even this is preferable to line management supervision or none at all.

Smaller agencies can often only offer supervision from paid workers who are also part of the management structure. This, for all the reasons outlined, is certainly not ideal. However difficulties can be minimized by careful thought and planning. The role of line manager needs to be carefully differentiated from that of counselling supervisor, although this necessitates the availability of at least two competent people. One offers counselling supervision to one set of counsellors, while the other offers line management to the same group and vice versa.

Agencies using outside supervisors arrange this variously. In some places the supervision is kept completely separate. Supervisors may or may not meet each other to discuss their work and support each other. They would only contact the agency if they had serious concerns about the competence of a supervisee or if they felt that proper ethical and professional standards were not being maintained. Other agencies have regular meetings of supervisors, with or without co-ordinators present. This would provide a forum for giving feedback to the agency on general matters relating to its organization and practice.

Finally, there is the question of the frequency of supervision. As the BAC *Code for Counsellors* states: 'The volume of supervision should be in proportion to the volume of counselling work undertaken and the experience of the counsellor' (BAC 1992: B.3.4). Unfortunately no other guidance is given by the BAC on what constitutes 'the proportion' in the equation of volume of counselling to supervision. The Association of Student Counselling (ASC) requires that 'consultations should take place preferably once a fortnight and should be an integral part of the counsellor's work' (ASC 1992: 2). However it does give more detailed guidelines on group supervision, which should be 'weekly for at least one and a half hours and preferably in a group of no more than four, so that each counsellor can present casework once a fortnight' (ASC 1992: 2). Naturally, agencies vary in the amount of supervision provided, but considering most volunteer counsellors do not have large case loads, usually between two to four clients per week, many agencies in reality are offering very favourable supervision/client ratios.

Group supervision has already been discussed and is frequently used in young people's counselling agencies. It is cost- and time-effective and also provides counsellors with peer support and its accompanying validation and challenge. It is also important to acknowledge that counsellors working for a few hours a week voluntarily enjoy an opportunity to meet colleagues that otherwise they would not meet. Signpost works to this model. Other agencies, like Centre 33 offer one-to-one supervision, but this is usually where counselling is just one service of a number offered in an agency. The counsellors may carry a higher case load but are too few or are not available at the same time to make group supervision viable. The better-funded agencies are more likely to offer both group and individual supervision. Thus the amount and type of supervision available to counsellors in young people's agencies may vary from very little supervision (fortunately this is rare), to group supervision offered fortnightly, three-weekly or monthly and/or individual supervision fortnightly or monthly. Some services arrange other support systems between counsellors which offer ongoing peer support. This is always as an adjunct to more formal counselling supervision.

In supervision, as in counselling, there are different models and ways of working which reflect the different theoretical orientations. For example, agencies which regard themselves as person-centred are more likely to offer that type of supervision. Where training is offered by the agency this opens up the possibility of experienced counsellors becoming supervisors. The style of supervision will then reflect the particular model of training. Other services which recruit from different counselling courses may be unable to provide supervision which is of the same theoretical model as the counsellors' original training. This can create difficulties for the counsellor, particularly where the language used by the supervisor is unfamiliar to the counsellor or understood within a different frame of reference. This is more likely for trainee or newly qualified counsellors rather than the more experienced, who are more likely to find the challenge of different approaches stimulating and thought-provoking, rather than potentially confusing and at worst undermining.

ASSESSMENT

In recent years greater emphasis has been placed on the monitoring and evaluating of services, particularly those services which are trying to attract and maintain funding. Assessment covers monitoring, evaluating and appraising both the service at large and the counselling within it. As we have seen, in many youth counselling agencies, once funding is achieved, it remains crucial to show that the money is being well used and that an effective service is provided. In addition to providing evidence to funders, this exercise can be a useful way of profiling a service and can stimulate new and creative ways of ensuring quality within the inevitable monetary restrictions.

The two main methods of monitoring are through the keeping of *statistics*, which allows for systematic data collection and analysis, and *quality assurance* which aims to monitor the quality of the service provided. Most young people's counselling services keep statistical data, but it is more likely to be within the county-funded youth counselling services that quality assurance is being promoted, as for example in Berkshire and Hertfordshire.

Counselling services usually keep two sources of statistics: those which record all the callers, either in person or on the phone, and those which are specifically related to people who make use of the counselling provision. In the first case the information collected would be fairly basic, such as geographical area, age, gender and source of referral. Once a client is seen by a counsellor more detailed information may be collated, such as ethnic origin, marital status and reason for coming. This last category can be very wide indeed, including all the problems and issues that are presented in counselling. These are valuable to the agency in promoting its effectiveness and demonstrating the wide range of difficulties young people can present with. They help to counteract the commonly held idea that young people do not encounter serious difficulties, merely experiencing relatively minor problems with peers. The reality is the converse: young people have identical concerns to adults, often further intensified by having less power than adults. This can be shocking to those who hold comfortable misconceptions. Abuse is just one example of the awful situations young people experience, and bullying and depression are others. Statistical data can be collected in a way that protects the identity of the client while providing valuable and powerful ammunition when fighting for resources and funding.

Quality assurance enables the service to be monitored by setting standards, aiming to meet them, and measuring performance once the service has been delivered. It is important to have objectives, strategies and performance indicators to measure the original objectives. For example, the time taken from initial contact to allocation to a counsellor can easily be measured, and is a useful indicator for assessing one aspect of service delivery effectiveness. User feedback is another way to find out and measure clients' feelings about the service provided, accessibility, the standard of premises etc. Supervision is an important arena for monitoring counsellor effectiveness in actual sessions. Appraisal enables both the counsellor and supervisor (or co-ordinator) to discuss and evaluate the counsellor's work. It also provides an opportunity to improve the quality of the service to clients by reviewing ongoing training needs, better ways of using supervision, and any means of encouraging the personal and professional development of the counsellor.

In this chapter we have explored the ways in which common counselling issues manifest themselves in work with young people. This client group, with their special vulnerabilities, presents counsellors with a particular challenge. They have to walk the line between acknowledging the autonomy and right to self-determination of their clients while at the same time recognizing and responding to young people's vulnerability. Counsellors have to operate within the framework of the laws on child protection, and of the policies of their employers. For all these reasons, counsellors working with young people need solid support and good quality supervision. In the next chapter we will go on to examine issues in counselling which are specific to work with this age group.

· FOUR ·

Specific issues in
counselling for young people

As well as the usual range of counselling skills, counsellors working
with the young need to have an understanding of the processes of
maturation and individuation to equip them for this work. Young
people will often act out within the counselling relationship the
challenging and confronting behaviour that is a part of growing up
and yet is experienced as negative and destructive by so many of
the adults with whom they come into contact. Counsellors need to
be aware not only of the likely manifestations of this behaviour but,
more importantly, of their own responses to it. In working with
young people it is vital to be responsive rather than reactive. This
is asking a great deal of counsellors, many of whom are in their
middle years and who may well be facing in the counselling situation very similar behaviour to that which drives them to despair
in their own families. This is yet another reason why support and
supervision are so important in providing counsellors with an opportunity to separate the personal from the professional, so that
they are able to function properly and provide a good service to
young people.

One response of young, distressed clients is to withdraw into
themselves and be silent. All counsellors need to be able to be
comfortable with silence because out of it new awareness or clari-
fication can come. However, there is another kind of silence in
which young clients are locked into themselves, and are unable or
unwilling to trust or to open up. How is the counsellor to respond?
Silences of this sort can often stretch the reserves of the counsellor
to breaking point. If left too long the silence becomes a battle of
wills, with the counsellor demonstrating the ability to tolerate the

silence and the client simply holding out. Clearly considerable skill is called for to recognize when to intervene and when to leave be.

It is important and helpful for the counsellor who is faced with this dilemma to remember the level of intrusion into their personal lives and feelings that some young people experience from adults, and to appreciate that for some the only way of maintaining any integrity or sense of themselves is to withdraw. Even if they have chosen to come into counselling, they may still act out this defence with their counsellors and it requires careful understanding and handling.

An example of how necessary it is for some young people to be allowed to be silent was a young woman from a very strict religious background who came into counselling because she was self-mutilating by cutting her arms and legs with razor blades. Her parents had taken her to the doctor, school psychologist, pastor and many other places for help. Eventually the young woman agreed to see a private counsellor on the understanding that there was to be no discussion within the family about the sessions.

She presented as rather an old-fashioned, mousy young woman, who after a polite hello would curl up in the counsellor's chair in an almost foetal position and say nothing. If spoken to she would respond politely but as briefly as possible. The exchange would go something like the following:

Counsellor: How are you feeling this week?
Client: The same as last week.
(Long silence)
Counsellor: What would you like to talk about today?
Client: I don't know.
(Long silence)

The counsellor did her best to ensure that her client was not feeling she had to be there, and also to reassure her about confidentiality. Paradoxically the client's behaviour demonstrated real commitment to the work. She never missed a session or came late and when it was time for the Christmas break she broke her silence to express anxiety about not being seen for two weeks, although needless to say she would not be drawn on this.

In the nine months that they met, the counsellor experienced a whole gamut of emotions which she steadfastly worked through in her supervision. At times she felt angry with and manipulated by her client. Often she experienced a crisis of confidence and a lack of trust in the process. Quite a lot of the time she felt bored. Most of the time she felt convinced that the silence of the client screamed out the depth of her distress and was unsure about how best to respond. She tried just to stay with the client, to be as congruent as possible and was constantly struggling with how much to intervene. After nine months the counselling ended at the client's request. As the last session drew to a close the client looked towards the counsellor and held eye contact, which was most unusual. She said quietly, 'I want to thank you very much for being here for me and for allowing me to be quiet.'

Some young people are withdrawn in the counselling situation because they feel out of their depth in the sphere of emotion. They do not feel confident about being able to express themselves when talking about their feelings. For others their past experience has taught them that their feelings will not be accepted or valued. It is only by allowing time for trust to be established and by respecting the client's pace that a therapeutic relationship can be developed with these young people. Others use silence as their only way of controlling the process in a world in which they rarely feel in control. For a few it is a passive way of expressing their resentment, hostility and aggression.

Adolescent clients may well present another kind of challenge to counsellors which is much less frequently encountered with an older client group. Some young people have come to regard all adults with suspicion and will act out their disaffection within the counselling. This may manifest itself by exhibiting a hostile or surly manner in the sessions or may be expressed more directly through challenging and confronting behaviour. It can be difficult, especially for the inexperienced counsellor, to stay with a client who seems to be constantly doubting their intentions and appears to be seeing the counsellor as part of the enemy.

Sometimes the behaviour may reflect a desire to shock and thus elicit and bring out into the open the disapproval that the client suspects to be within the counsellor. The client may describe behaviour that they suspect will be offensive to the counsellor. For example, a young male client was seeing a woman counsellor in an agency which prided itself on its equal opportunities policy. The counsellor herself was a feminist. The young man would relate his treatment of his girlfriends to the counsellor, speaking of them in very derogatory tones. He would describe incidents where he had acted violently towards them and imply that they deserved this abuse. The other side of the coin was that he lived with his mother who had been abandoned by his father and who acted out much of her anger on her son, claiming that he was 'just like his father'.

The counsellor had to establish a relationship with this young man in which he felt valued, respected and able to trust. She had to cope with his ambivalence towards women and with his transferred anger. If she was to be congruent she also had to find a way to challenge his behaviour and his attitudes, which were causing him problems and making it impossible for him to form relationships, but she had to do so in a way which he would not experience as a rejection and a fulfilment of his prophecy. The young man needed to feel that it was his behaviour that was being challenged and not his very being. Once he felt safe within the relationship he was able to show his pain, vulnerability, fear and also his gentleness and caring.

Counsellors working with young adolescents or those who are relatively immature especially need to have and to demonstrate a flexibility of approach. Clients who are not able to articulate their feelings in words might be able to use drawings or other media as a way into their work. The language of feelings may not be readily available to some and so it is possible that the level of intervention required will be greater than it might be with older clients. The teaching and practising of interpersonal skills, such as assertiveness, might be appropriate within the sessions, for example with a client who was being bullied. All in all, it is unlikely that a rigid and dogmatic adherence to any system of working will be useful. It is certainly not realistic to expect a young and inexperienced client to be able either to enter the relationship as an equal or to launch into the work with only a modicum of help.

No two young people develop and mature at the same rate. A variety of factors – physical, emotional, social and familial – will affect this process. A counsellor working with the young will need to be sensitive to each young person individually. Adolescent behaviour and bravado are clearly linked and clients may be ashamed of their insecurity and their inexperience. For example, a youth worker was working with a group of young men who were very vociferous about their sexual conquests. The most physically mature member of this group was a very attractive young man who was loud and boastful in his stories and said to have no feelings at all for the young women whom he claimed were his prey. However, when he communicated on a one-to-one basis he was very different. In a session with the youth worker he expressed considerable anxiety about something which he implied was of a sexual nature. The youth worker's imagination ran riot. Had he been having unprotected sex and caught some infection? Was he gay? Had he been abused? After much encouragement and endless guarantees of confidentiality he finally confided in the youth worker that he was helplessly in love with someone and was terribly worried because he was not sure if he knew how to kiss properly. The worker learned from this the folly of making assumptions about the level of development of the young people with whom he worked. Bravado often covers both inexperience and anxiety and can further alienate the adult world from the young.

All counsellors have to be willing to enter into their clients' world in order to understand their world view and their assumptions. In working with the young, counsellors will often find that the world view of their clients is challenging to their own. For example, it is all too easy for the counsellor to dismiss the young client's idealism as naïvety and to forget the importance of that idealism to the developmental process. Furthermore, it is not comfortable to acknowledge the mess our own generation has made of the world and the legacy we leave to the next generation. The work that young clients bring may demand that counsellors do just that. The young can face the adult world with uncomfortable truths and realities that are generally denied or simply not seen.

Some appreciation of youth culture in general is helpful but it is even more important to understand the client's particular cultural and social context. The pressure on the young to conform to peer group norms is enormous, seeming like a matter of survival to many. Counsellors need to be aware of this to be able to appreciate the dilemmas facing young people.

Counsellors of young people need to avoid acting in a parental way with their clients. Needy young people can easily evoke a maternal or paternal feelings in their counsellors. Rebellious and provocative young clients can evoke disapproval. These feelings, though understandable, are not appropriate to the counselling relationship.

The majority of young people who come into counselling will either be living, or have recently been living, as part of a family. In attempting to understand young people's distress and its manifestations it is important to remember that they may well be a part of a family unit that is itself dysfunctional. Children of dysfunctional families often end up carrying the sickness that rightly belongs in the family unit. One member, frequently a young person, is scapegoated into being the 'problem' or may take on being the problem in order to unify warring parents. Tragically, some young people end up sacrificing themselves to hold the family together. For example, a young woman client had for years tolerated regular sexual assault and rape by her father in order to prevent her younger sisters from becoming his victims, her mother from being hurt and her family from being broken up. She took pride in this sacrifice and only sought help when it became clear that she could no longer divert her father's attentions from one of her younger sisters.

Destructive patterns of behaviour and ways of relating in the young most often have at root a dysfunctional family where they are learned. Young people are physically, emotionally and often financially dependent on these families and are unlikely to be autonomous individuals within them. Those who have left either by choice or because they have finally been rejected have to deal with the unfinished business that remains. Counsellors need to bear in mind that the pathology young people display may be carried by them but belong to the family. The task for some young people is to learn a whole new way of being which is a long and difficult task. The counselling relationship itself, characterized by mutual respect and equality, can be a model for this new way of being and provide the forum in which to begin to learn it.

STRESSES AND SATISFACTIONS IN COUNSELLING YOUNG PEOPLE

While there is much job satisfaction to be gained from counselling young people, it is important to acknowledge that the work can also be very stressful. To survive in it one needs resilience, endless patience and a lively sense of humour. Young clients are notorious for missing appointments and failing to get in touch. While it is important to reflect on this in the work and look out for reasons for this, it should be balanced by not taking this behaviour personally and recognizing that the young tend to live in the moment and that yesterday's crisis is soon forgotten. A young person can quite genuinely and normally be distraught about the ending of a romance on Monday and enthusiastically into a new one by Friday. This is not to underrate their feelings in any way but it can explain the common phenomenon of a client coming in to an agency and demanding an urgent appointment with a counsellor and then failing to keep it or of just not turning up for a session when the work seems to have been going well. Counsellors do need to be able to tolerate and understand this apparently casual approach.

Much of the work with the young is short-term, often crisis intervention work, which many counsellors find less rewarding than longer-term counselling. The counsellor may be left not knowing the outcome of the intervention or fearing that while the crisis has been dealt with the underlying problem remains untouched. We have to learn to stand back and trust the process and clients' right to choose when they will address their issues, understanding that at this point in their development young people may only be able to take the first steps in what may ultimately be a long journey. Counsellors need to value the importance of these steps. If young people have a positive experience of counselling at this stage, they are more likely to return later in life and take up the journey again.

Counsellors working with the young have to appreciate that their clients may not be autonomous. Young people are often given very little say in where and how the family lives and their freedom and options are restricted. Sometimes it is not within their power to change or leave a difficult or painful situation. Young adolescents in particular are often faced with learning to live with something as their only option. Even their rights as clients may be challenged. Parents or other professionals may feel they have a right to be party to the counselling itself and to exercise some control over what is discussed and the outcome. This is obviously very difficult and threatening for young people and is also stressful and problematic for counsellors trying to do their work in these circumstances. Not only are they working with the client but are also having to withstand a good deal of anger and resentment from others for refusing to collude with their inappropriate request for information.

However, there can be little doubt of the satisfaction to be gained from watching young clients grow, develop and find their power in the world. Their energy, enthusiasm and potential is inspiring, as is their ability to cope with adversity and find a way of moving through it. Counsellors working with the young are often privileged to see the shift from boy to young man or girl to young woman. They are witness to them becoming aware of their rights and responsibilities as human beings. They see them growing in confidence as they absorb these rights and responsibilities, thus becoming the authors of their own lives and their own future.

SETTING UP A COUNSELLING SERVICE FOR YOUNG PEOPLE

The following constitute what we consider to be the minimum requirements for setting up an adequate counselling service for young people in a school or community setting.

Needs analysis

Prior to establishing a service it is important to ask two pertinent questions:

Is there a perceived need by young people for such a service?
Is this need being met in any other form in the vicinity or elsewhere?

The involvement of young people in surveys demonstrates, perhaps not surprisingly, that their needs are a microcosm of the needs of adults in the population. Young people state that they want services such as the Citizens Advice Bureau, health clinics, and other specialized and accessible services which focus specifically and non-clinically on the needs of young people. Thus the answer to the first question is that invariably there is a need for a service, and to the second that although generally there are some services, these are not geared to young people.

When young people are asked what they want, the most frequent request is that services should be available under one roof. This is difficult to provide in a school setting but more possible within a community-based service. As we have seen in Chapter 2, this type of service can respond to the needs of young people as they arise and can be specifically tailored to the particular difficulties or issues that emerge in the specific area, whether urban or rural. In response to these, decisions can be made regarding the type of service it is appropriate to offer. This could include information, advice, advocacy, befriending and emergency accommodation. If counselling is one of the services offered, it is important to decide how this is to be defined. An important question is whether counselling consists of workers using counselling skills in an informal setting, or formal counselling which requires a contract between counsellor and client.

Setting

A basic requirement of any counselling is an appropriate-sized room, which is both private and interruption-free and where a level of anonymity can be maintained. In a school this means somewhere discreet, away from both the staffroom and main pupil thoroughfare. In a youth club this would be a room used only outside of normal hours to ensure confidentiality. Where space allows, some services are able to provide a special counselling suite separate from other facilities, which is ideal. Rooms need to be suitably furnished and checked for sound-proofing. There is nothing more inhibiting to both counsellor and client than to hear voices in the corridor, or loud music from the common room or see writing on the blackboard.

New initiatives in rural areas have included the use of buses or vans as places for offering counselling. Although it is important to make services accessible, the lack of both privacy and confidentiality is a significant issue and one not easily solved. Discreet parking and curtains can help.

In our experience, community-based counselling services are well advised to have more than one room available. It is never advisable to have counsellors working alone and it is much more time- and personnel-effective to have a reception worker for two counsellors rather than one. Additionally, if one person goes sick, or is on holiday, there is always someone else available.   ˙

Recruitment and selection

Qualities that are essential for working with young people are flexibility, openness to challenge, and an ability to establish real empathic contact quickly, as well as a sense of fun. Young people as a client group are much more likely to vote with their feet if the contact seems in any way unreal, patronizing or otherwise inappropriate. It is essential that counsellors are highly aware of their own attitudes with regard to equal opportunities. They need to be personally committed to non-discriminatory practice. The agency needs to support them by providing training and by creating an atmosphere in which no one is complacent about their attitudes, everyone is willing to make and receive challenges and equal opportunities is always on the agenda.

Not all clients will be able to come to a counselling service, especially if they do not wish their parents to know. This has meant that counsellors will sometimes have to go to the client – for instance, seeing a young person in the school if a suitable setting is available. In some rural areas, telephone counselling has been the only possible alternative for a young person. Therefore a flexibility in attitude is also an important requirement of potential counsellors for this age group if this form of help is to be genuinely accessible.

The recruitment of staff also needs to reflect the ethnic mix of the area. It is not uncommon for Asian and Afro-Caribbean young people to request a black counsellor, and many agencies prioritize the recruitment of counsellors to reflect these requirements. This is also true of recruiting male and female counsellors, although it is sometimes important to gently challenge requests by young men for a female counsellor when it is couched in terms of 'only women can really listen'. One male counsellor, after a few months working in a young people's service, began to wonder if he would ever see a client as all the requests the previous month had been for female counsellors! Ultimately it is important to listen to what clients are asking for and make efforts to respond.

Selection of counsellors is an important process. Not everyone is necessarily suited to work with young people, especially if they do not have the prerequisite qualities mentioned above. It can be very stressful working with young people who can be very challenging, or who may spend session after session in almost total silence. These areas need to be addressed at the initial interview. Often counsellors will decide, especially if they are in training, to try a different client group. Selection needs to be even more rigorous for services training their own counsellors. Training costs money and agencies need to be as sure as possible that they will get a return on the investment.

Although within the framework of a school, counsellors would normally be paid, in the community it is rare to find paid counsellors, unless they are attached to a particular project employing them specifically to work with young people. The only staff who are paid in the voluntary sector are the managers or co-ordinators of the service. Some may carry a client case load but normally managerial responsibilities, liaison, and management committee work makes this impossible. Despite the fact that most counsellors at best receive only travel expenses, commitment is not usually an issue and many agencies have a waiting list of people wishing to volunteer their services. There are two main reasons for this. First, some young people's counselling services – for example Off the Record, Number 5 and Share – offer counselling training which is usually free. Second, services that recruit from counselling courses are often inundated by students requiring placements, especially if these offer supervision and training opportunities.

Training

We would challenge the assumption that only the lowest level of counselling training is required to work with young people. There is still a tendency to think that all social workers, teachers or youth workers can counsel. They may make good use of listening and basic counselling skills, but this does not mean they are trained in counselling. Ideally counsellors trained to high level would be employed, whether that is through in-service training programmes or recruiting from outside courses. The introduction of NVQs (National Vocational Qualifications) may be a way to increase the availability of counselling qualifications for people from a variety of backgrounds, and this is discussed in Chapter 6.

It is important that counsellors have access to in-service training wherever they work, as it allows them an opportunity to reflect on their work, which is essential to the counselling process. In-house training needs to be properly budgeted and must include an element of equal opportunities training. However, it is often training which is the first to go when funding is cut, to the detriment of both client and counsellor.

Supervision

As we saw in the previous chapter, this should ideally be non-managerial and brought in from outside. It should be regular and a requirement for all counsellors to attend. It also needs to be appropriate to the level of work undertaken by the agency and individual counsellors. When setting up a service it is useful to liaise with existing services which may be able to offer some supervision or consultancy. Child and family clinics or local college counselling services are often good starting places for mutual contact, referral, and even supervision because professionals working in these places will be experienced in working with young people.

Referral

Referral can be a potentially difficult area when working with young people, whether within the school or the community. Wherever possible it is always preferable for the young person to self-refer even if they have been 'advised' to by a teacher or other agency. However even in these cases it is not unknown for young people to arrive for counselling inferring that they have been 'sent' and not really knowing why they are there. If this occurs it is important for the counsellor to work with this and renegotiate the contract making sure the young person has the choice to stay or not. In most cases they do continue once they realize this. Occasionally they choose to leave, but it is not unusual for them to return at a future time if their experience was positive and they felt no pressure.

In our experience more and more agencies are referring young people for counselling, partly because the effectiveness of this way of working is increasingly being recognized, and partly because other professionals – social workers, teachers, the Careers Service – do not have the time or the expertise to offer ongoing counselling. Now that counselling has become relatively common within medical practice, more GPs are willing to refer to recognized agencies and they are becoming a major source of referral. Referrals from other professionals are usually well handled. The referrer may make the initial contact, followed either by the young person making and attending the appointment or the professional concerned bringing them to the first session if they need support. If this occurs, generally they will not remain in the counselling room with the client, although they will occasionally if there is a language difficulty or a disability that needs the presence of a third party.

Parent referrals are often more difficult. Many parents are concerned with the behaviour of their son or daughter and contact counselling agencies to make appointments for their child. Some agencies will not work in this way, whereas others will see parents and take referrals from them if it is ascertained that the young person is part of the process and that the parent is merely making the initial contact. On these occasions it is common for the agency to write to the young person offering them an appointment but leaving it to them to confirm, making it clear that coming or not is their choice. It can be the parent and not the young person who has the difficulty. In these cases agencies who offer counselling to parents can encourage the parent to come in to explore different ways of being with the young person as well as offering them emotional support. This can be a very effective way of working on the behalf of young people without ever seeing them. Quite often parents see certain types of behaviour as problematic and are relieved to find that it is not unusual but a normal part of the process of moving towards independence and autonomy.

Responsibility for the service and its management

Responsibility for the service and its management should be clearly defined and understood by everyone in it. In a school it is important for the counsellors to know to whom they are responsible, both for line management and in relation to issues of child protection. A community service will have a management committee which is usually made up of representatives from outside organizations and internal representatives from the agency and, ideally, young people. It carries the ultimate responsibility for the work of the service both to the funding authorities and internally to staff. Thus there is a two-way responsibility and accountability within the organization. Staff are accountable to the clients who receive their service and to the agency, which is often represented by a management committee which employs them in either a paid or a voluntary capacity. All staff need representation on the management committee, preferably through an elected representative for counsellors and/or other service staff. Managers or co-ordinators of the service are sometimes line managed through the major funding body, for example Youth and Community or Social Services, others purely through their management committee. In the former case there are implications in this type of arrangement because the agency is then under the direct responsibility of a particular county council authority, which may mean limitations on confidentiality offered to young people. Agencies who do not have direct responsibility to funders are often able to offer total confidentiality according to their own guidelines, as NAYPCAS recommends (Lawton 1980: C8).

It is essential for a youth counselling agency to clarify the lines of responsibility on such matters as line management, supervision, and child protection. In order to do this a programme of induction is invaluable, as is a written document covering these procedures. Documentation should also exist for equal opportunities, codes of ethics and practice, counselling ethos, disciplinary and grievance procedures for staff and clients, and health, safety and security guidelines. These should be written in an accessible style, be readily and easily available and regularly updated if they are to be effective.

Reports

Report writing as a means of keeping other professionals and the public informed is essential. This can be achieved in a variety of ways. Annual reports are probably the way most services publicize their activities. These will contain details of the services on offer by the agency and a statistical breakdown of their use. This would include usage by young people, parents and other professionals. Co-ordinators' reports to management committees are also an important way of publicizing the service as these are usually made up of representatives from interested and influential organizations, such as Social and Careers Services, local schools, libraries, education and the police. These services receive reports made to committee meetings through their constituent members informing them of the activities of the agency and the needs it caters for.

Recording, monitoring and evaluating

It is essential to monitor the use of the service; partly to ensure its effectiveness in meeting the needs of young people, and partly as a way of showing funders or potential funders how the service is currently being used. This is done by collecting and analysing statistical information and by ensuring there is a system of quality assurance and user feedback. The latter may be collected on an *ad hoc* basis from clients' comments to their counsellor, or through optional clients' exit forms. These are anonymous and ask for comments or assessments by the client on the effectiveness of the counselling, the accessibility of the agency, comfort offered in the premises, and anything else the agency may wish to know about.

Another important reason for monitoring the use of the service is to identify to what extent minority groups are being served. This may raise questions such as are there any black or Asian counsellors? Is the service geared to meeting the needs of young people with a disability? It is not unusual for services to have a predominance of white middle-class, heterosexual women. An audit of background of sex, sexual orientation and ethnicity is an important way to monitor how the counsellors and agency appear to the community outside. An interesting result of a language audit in Signpost was to bring to light the variety of languages that could be offered, up to then unrecognized. These included Urdu, Punjabi, Bengali, Italian, Hungarian, French, Danish, Spanish and Polish.

Accessibility

This includes both physical access, ambience, attractiveness to young people and position, as well as factors mentioned above, such as staffing, that could affect a young person's attitude towards using the service.

Few services have had significant funding to provide purpose-built accommodation. Some agencies have had parts of the building designed particularly for their needs, such as Signpost in Watford or the YEIS (Youth Enquiry and Information Service) shop in Stevenage. Even then, the original building is not particularly welcoming or is not situated in the most accessible place for young people. Often budgets have been small so that any conversions of existing premises are not ideal or have been designed by people who have little concept of what is required for a counselling and information service.

Some of the most welcoming places are converted family houses in quiet side streets off the town centre, although disabled access and parking may be difficult. On the one hand a quiet street may seem fairly anonymous for users compared to a busy shop front agency in the High Street; on the other it is less likely to be known and young people going for evening appointments on their own may feel vulnerable.

Each agency has to weigh up the advantages and disadvantages of different sites, according to the service it wishes to offer, the area it is servicing and the young people whose needs it is trying to meet. Young people, like any other group of individuals, will have different tastes so that whereas one group may suggest a bright colourful environment within the building, another group may prefer a more homely, conventional type of surrounding. Whatever the preferences, it is essential that young people's counselling services are easily accessible to bus routes and are within easy and safe walking distance of these. Young people, unlike adult users of similar services, are highly unlikely to have their own transport.

Finally, it is essential that systems are put in place which guarantee that young people are seen quickly and not interviewed and then put on to a waiting list, as is the case with most services to adults. Young people would find it difficult or impossible to fit into this model.

Conclusion

The areas we have discussed above only constitute the significant factors which need to be addressed when considering setting up a counselling agency for young people. Most agencies only offer counselling as one service among others, so it is also important to decide how the counselling will be integrated within the total organization. If information is one of the services, an invaluable source of reference is provided by the National Youth Agency (NYA) in its booklet *The Information Shop Specification* (McDonald 1990). It is the result of consultations with young people as well as with workers from existing counselling and information services (see Chapter 1). However much of the material has a wider relevance and is a valuable and useful starting point for any group considering the practicalities of setting up services for young people.

· FIVE ·

Professional relationships in counselling for young people

There are several important issues involved in working with other professionals, within agencies, schools, and in other settings. Counselling is still perceived by some professionals as either suspect and threatening or as an easy option that requires no specific training. Establishing good working relationships within which the counselling process is understood and valued is extremely important if counsellors are to work alongside others in the provision of the best possible service to young people.

There is a fundamental difference between counselling and other ways of helping young people. It is this difference that causes many of the misunderstandings that occur. It is the difference between *doing* and *being*. Most social work interventions involve doing something on behalf of or with the client. Similarly, teaching is generally an activity where the teacher controls the agenda with a distinct outcome in mind. Counselling is not about doing or action, it is about *being with*, a concept that is paradoxically both simple and profound. Other professionals whose mind set is different, whose focus is on doing, may well end up undervaluing the counselling process, which does not involve doing and whose outcome is difficult to quantify. The unstructured space offered by the counselling process is itself threatening to those who are not familiar with it because it provides a forum for the expression of young people's pain and distress about the circumstances of their lives and thus conflicts with the need of adults to silence the young.

If *doing* is the focus, then merely *being with* may be seen as somehow not a legitimate enterprise. Counsellors working with other professionals will be familiar with the claim that anyone, given the luxury of a one-to-one situation and an hour of time, could help the young person sort out their problems. This is a defensive response which denies the fact that counsellors bring a special and particular set of skills and way of being to that situation which have a profound effect on the inherent dynamics and on the nature of the interaction. It is one way of helping among many that can certainly complement the others but may occasionally clash with them.

In addition, young people who are the clients of social workers are likely to be in that situation because of a set of circumstances over which they have no control or because they have fallen foul of the law. Young people, under the age of 16, have to attend school. The clients of counsellors working with young people have actively chosen to be clients, which alters the dynamic and the power balance within the relationship.

WORKING WITH TEACHERS

Teachers, working a full timetable and struggling to meet the ever-increasing demands made upon them, such as educational testing and the imposition of the National Curriculum, can be forgiven for sometimes viewing counselling as an easy and much less demanding option. Most of them struggle throughout their working lives to provide a caring and humane environment and to meet the needs of the children they teach. Unfortunately work pressure and time constraints mean they rarely give the time and attention to the pastoral needs of the children that they might otherwise wish to, however much they try to prioritize this. This dynamic sometimes has the unfortunate consequence of setting up a kind of professional jealousy towards the work of counsellors which can be destructive and unhelpful to all concerned. (The difficulties and dilemmas facing counsellors working in schools have been discussed at some length in Chapter 2.)

In addition, because counsellors often end up working with young people who may be perceived by other staff as difficult and uncooperative, the counselling process is sometimes viewed as a cop out. Instead of being properly disciplined the young person is being counselled. The image of the counsellor as a woolly liberal, naïve and unable to see through the offender, is more common than most of us care to admit. Those unfamiliar with the counselling process will not be aware of its often confrontational nature or of its inherent purpose, which is to encourage these young clients to take responsibility for their part in the difficulties and problems in their lives.

There is another very sensitive dynamic at play between teachers and counsellors working together. The relationship between teachers and students is similar to that between counsellor and client in two significant ways although very different in others – firstly by its inherent power dynamic and secondly by being conducted largely in private, that is, away from the gaze of other adults or professionals. Teachers, like counsellors, are generally people of integrity who work hard to do their jobs as well and as ethically as possible. However in teaching, as in counselling, there is a small minority whose practice is suspect and would not stand up to scrutiny. Counsellors working in schools or other agencies offering a confidential service and willing to listen to young people can hear information about bad or suspect practice on the part of a particular teacher. Even teachers whose practice is extremely ethical may well fear that information given to the counsellor is inevitably one-sided and from the student's perspective only, and may mean that they are harshly judged or misunderstood. For many teachers, used to working behind closed classroom doors, the whole concept of scrutiny is difficult and unfamiliar and in this particular instance they are unlikely to be able to put forward their point of view.

This dynamic needs to be recognized and acknowledged by both sets of professionals as there are no easy solutions. The work of a counsellor employed in a large sixth-form college demonstrates the difficulties that can arise. Over the course of several years and through working with many students, she became increasingly concerned about a particular member of staff. Many young women expressed discomfort about the way he would lean over them or put his arm around them. Students of both sexes complained about his attitudes which they perceived to be sexist, racist and homophobic. On one occasion, a young woman student came to a session dressed in a way that the counsellor felt was quite inappropriate for college. She did not express this to the student, but was told in the course of the hour that she had worn these particular clothes because she wanted to maximize the marks she would be awarded for a presentation she had to give to a group taught by this man.

While there was much in his behaviour that was questionable, students felt powerless and unwilling to challenge a senior member of staff. Although his attitudes and behaviour were offensive it was arguable as to whether or not he transgressed any ethical or professional codes. Staff were almost evenly divided between those who felt he was the salt of the earth and those who found him patronizing and offensive.

The counsellor, after consultation with her supervisor, spoke to the head of the school in general terms, who although expressing concern, said she was unable to act unless she had a student or students willing to make and substantiate a complaint. She did however speak to the man, which resulted in his becoming openly hostile to the counsellor and strongly advising his students to have nothing to do with her. Nothing was resolved and the situation continued. Fortunately this kind of situation is rare, but when it occurs counsellors have to find a way to work with it and a satisfactory outcome cannot be guaranteed.

WORKING WITH SOCIAL WORKERS

Although most social work training now includes interpersonal and counselling skills, this does not qualify a person to be a counsellor. Social workers are constrained by their statutory obligations with regard to clients and their families, so it is particularly difficult for them to create and maintain the appropriate therapeutic relationship required for counselling. In common with nurses, many social workers who come into counselling training initially find it difficult to give up the intervention model. They are highly trained in assessment, in making judgements of client needs, advising, advocating and in a whole variety of other skills. However their role, arising from legal and societal expectations, makes working in the counselling mode, without an agenda, almost impossible. In our experience once social workers and counsellors have worked together, they quickly become aware of how their roles complement one another, but trust and an understanding of each other's working practices needs to be established.

Despite the huge amount of evidence, society finds it hard to come to terms with the fact that throughout the ages and across all cultures some children and young people have been hurt, abused, misused and even killed by the adults who are supposed to be taking care of them. Instead of addressing the issues of violence, neglect and abuse of power inherent in this problem, society has put its energy into apportioning blame: social workers are constantly scapegoated when something goes wrong. One positive outcome of this unfortunate situation is that child protection procedures have been tightened up considerably and practice has consequently improved. It has, however, left many social workers feeling understandably nervous and desiring to be in control of what they may ultimately be blamed for.

Counsellors offering young people confidentiality can be perceived as a threat in that they may be exercising their discretion over what information is being passed on to social workers. Child protection issues in counselling are discussed later in this chapter, but suffice it to say at this point that counsellors are also constrained in what they may and may not do. The best way forward is by forming good working relationships between the two professions.

An example of a project in which social workers and counsellors were working in tandem came about in response to a particularly harrowing case of a child prostitution ring. Young people of both sexes from the age of 10 to 16 were involved, many of whom were either runaways or in care. Once the arrests were made and the legal proceedings set in motion, a team of social workers and counsellors started working. The social workers took responsibility for care arrangements where appropriate, for getting the young people back into education or employment and for negotiating the welfare benefits system for those who needed it. The counsellors were available to both the young people and their parents to address the emotional and personal effects of what had happened. The work was long-term and a system was set in place to deal with child protection issues, particularly with regard to new disclosures. Some group work was offered to the young people and eventually a youth worker became involved. Educational welfare officers and teachers were enlisted to smooth the process of returning to education for some of the young people. All the professionals concerned, but particularly the counsellors and social workers who had been involved from the outset, gained a great deal from this partnership.

WORKING WITH YOUTH WORKERS

Modern youth work has its emphasis on social education, as opposed to the mere provision of leisure activity and the exercise of social control. As a result there has been a move away from centre-based provision to a style of work that is much more responsive to the self-defined needs of young people, which includes project and outreach work. Many youth workers subsequently undertake further training in counselling and work in youth agencies that provide counselling. Most other youth workers use counselling skills with their client group but few receive the kind of supervision and training that would support this aspect of their work.

Youth workers and counsellors often find themselves in the unfortunate position of competing for ever-shrinking resources. This pressure can be divisive and encourages competition rather than co-operation. In addition, the very nature of youth work requires a flexible approach to boundary issues and a willingness to constantly re-establish and redefine these. This is paradoxically its greatest strength and its greatest weakness. At best, this leads to creative and inspiring work but at worst youth workers become somewhat un-reliable, anarchic and difficult to work with. Counsellors have a different approach to boundaries because of their importance within the therapeutic relationship, and this can sometimes appear to be rigid.

An example of this difference came to light between a youth worker and a counsellor who were working with the same client. This client was a notoriously bad timekeeper. She expressed a strong desire to see the counsellor, which was arranged with the help of the youth worker, who brought the client to the first session where the contract and boundaries were clearly defined with her. Never-theless she was half an hour late for her next session and was quite indignant when the counsellor brought the session to a close on time. She complained to the youth worker, who rang the counsellor asking for a second appointment that week, explaining the circum-stances of the client's lateness. The counsellor said she was not able to discuss the matter with her and suggested that she asked the client to ring in person. The youth worker felt a little offended by this. The client did keep the next appointment and arrived on time but was 40 minutes late for the third appointment. The counsellor kept to the boundary and the client left very angry and unwilling to return.

When they next met the youth worker explained her perception of the situation. She felt that the young person had a lot of issues to work through and had been prevented from doing so by the rigidity of the counsellor. The counsellor's perception was that the young person had not kept to the contract she had freely entered into, her lateness was an issue in itself and that to collude with it would be counter-productive and patronizing to the client. They tried hard to see each other's point of view and agreed to differ.

WORKING WITH OTHER SERVICES

In addition to schools and the voluntary sector, there are a number of agencies offering young people counselling and related services, such as telephone counselling and issue-based self-help groups. These agencies complement and support the work of the more main-stream services because they offer expertise in specific areas of work.

We have selected four services of the many available to illustrate the diversity of response to young people's distress.

Childline

An important contribution to young people's counselling is made by the charity Childline. Launched in 1986 by Esther Rantzen, it provides a telephone counselling service 24 hours a day. This is a free national helpline for children in trouble or danger. While its headquarters are in Islington, there are additional services in Nottingham, Glasgow, Manchester, Swansea and Rhyl. Calls from children in those areas go through to the local service during peak hours, while at other times calls are diverted to London.

British Telecom provides the London building and the lines. The money to run the service is raised by a network of Friends of Childline. Grants, trusts and corporate support are also an important source of revenue. From each £1 raised 79p is used for counselling, 9p for support services and 12p for fundraising. Childline have also piloted a Children-in-Care line, specifically for young people experiencing difficulties in residential homes and hostels. There was a similar one for those in boarding schools, and a bullying line. They are not ongoing owing to cost, but have provided important statistics and information about young people in difficulty. Advocacy is an important part of Childline's work, bringing the public's attention to issues affecting children's welfare and rights. For example, one role Childline is able to fulfil is presenting records, taken by the counsellor with the child's permission, in court in cases of abuse.

The counsellors are all volunteers and over 450 are employed in answering calls. There are no specific criteria for recruitment of volunteers but all go through the same training course. Information meetings are held every four to six weeks for potential volunteers to hear more about the organization, the work involved, and to watch a video of the service in action. Forms are available for those still interested and are aimed to encourage the would-be counsellor to look at their life experience and motives for wanting to be involved. Over 70 per cent are selected for interview and this will be followed by a training course of 10 weeks, a total of 35 hours. Approximately 83 per cent of trainees will be successful and continue to do a further three administrative sessions. They deal with note-taking, policy and practice. This is followed by three observation periods where the volunteer shadows a 'buddy' who allows time to talk through issues arising from calls and the volunteer's anxieties. Finally after 16 weeks the new counsellor is able to start work on one of the six four-hour shifts.

Supervision is every six weeks in groups of up to six. Although this seems rather infrequent, supervisors are available on every shift and there is a half-hour debriefing between shifts. The 'volunteer development officer' is available for ongoing support for new counsellors. All volunteers meet regularly to discuss issues of concern, such as frequency of supervision and the arrangement of the 'counselling room' (a large office where the volunteers answer the phone).

Calls are constantly coming in and are monitored by a computerized switchboard indicating lines that are free. Lines are open on the basis of one per counsellor and one extra. Calls unable to be answered receive a taped message from Esther Rantzen to try again, or are put on hold waiting for the next counsellor to be free. There are 15 lines available but rarely enough counsellors to staff them. Approximately 10,000 calls come through each day and about 2,700 are answered (27 per cent). One of the difficulties is recruiting enough volunteers and keeping them once recruited. Although Childline does try and support its counsellors, many can feel overwhelmed by the volume and severe nature of the calls. Physical and sexual abuse are the two largest issues, although domestic violence and difficulties between family members is frequent (Childline 1993). We feel that if the training for counsellors was longer and supervision more frequent the drop-out rate would be less. Not everyone feels able to ask for support from supervisors on shift or during the handover, while the highly stressful nature of this type of counselling does require counsellors to feel confident in their ability to cope.

However, there is no doubt that Childline provides a vital service to young people, and its high profile in the public eye guarantees it constant funding compared to other young people's services. Childline does refer out to other agencies those young people prepared to use them, but the anonymity offered by Childline is one of its greatest strengths.

Agony aunts

At the launch of Youth Access in January 1993 14 agony aunts and one agony uncle were invited to take part in the new profile Youth Access was promoting. They represented both newspapers and magazines, for example, Deidre Sanders (*Sun*), Ann Lovell (*Bella*), Vicky Maud (*True Story* and *True Romance*) and Nick Fisher (*Just 17*). Like Childline, the relative anonymity of writing to someone for advice is particularly attractive to young people. The agony aunts report that they are receiving an increased volume of letters relating to subjects such as drugs and pregnancy from young people. In their replies they often suggest counselling to their young writer,

and refer them to their local youth counselling service. The importance of their work is easily overlooked.

Relateteen

Relateteen was an initiative coming out of the Northern Ireland
branch of Relate. In the late eighties concern was mounting for the
children of broken relationships. With funding from the Department of Health and the Children in Need Appeal, Relateteen came
into being. It was officially launched by the Princess of Wales in
December 1993 but the pilot scheme had been running for about
three years before then.

Its aim is to provide counselling to young people roughly between
the ages of 12 and 18 whose lives have been affected by the breakup
of their parents' relationship. The team of counsellors was selected
for its suitability for work with young people, having come from
either a counselling or a social work background. The participants
all then took part in Relateteen's own training programme which
is specially designed to prepare the counsellors for working with
this age group. Supervision, support and ongoing training is provided by the project.

Clients either self-refer or are referred by their parents or other
concerned adults. The young clients are not asked to pay for this
service but the organization welcomes any contribution that the
referring adult feels able to make.

It is very common for the children of broken relationships to
imagine that they themselves are responsible for the difficulties at
home and the end of the relationship. Others feel that they must
take responsibility for their younger siblings or even for the parent
remaining at home who may be emotionally distressed and not
coping too well. Relateteen offers these young people an opportunity
to talk through the implications of the partnership breakdown both
for the family and for themselves and to express their own feelings
about it which may have been ignored. As two of the service users
have commented:

> During a marriage breakup the needs of the children are nor-
> mally forgotten about, very few people actually realize how
> we feel or how the break up is affecting us.

> I was able to see that I couldn't solve my parents' problems
> and that I didn't need to feel guilty about it.

This initiative has been so successful that other Relate groups are
about to embark on similar schemes.

Alateen

Alateen is an offshoot of Al-Anon, a world-wide organization offering support to the families and friends of problem drinkers. While it does not offer counselling as such, it provides an opportunity for young people between the ages of 12 and 20 to meet in self-help groups supported by the organization. In addition, young people in distress needing someone to talk to about problem drinking in the family can telephone the organization and speak to someone who has had similar experiences in his or her life. The first Alateen group was established in Britain in 1964.

Other workers rarely understand the level of accountability young people's counselling services have to meet. The political climate is so divisive that professions can fall into the trap of being defensive about their own work and critical of others. Myths abound and are rarely challenged, for example the idea that teachers work short hours and have endless holidays, that social workers interfere with good families and miss the ones in crisis and that counsellors are woolly liberals issuing nothing but tea and sympathy. Other professionals can make strange bedfellows but it is important to remember that we are all on the same side.

Whatever the setting, there are three areas where conflict is likely to arise between counsellors and other professionals working with young people. These are contract and agenda setting, confidentiality and funding.

CONTRACT AND AGENDA SETTING

Where other professionals have referred clients to a counsellor, they may expect both some say in the agenda for the work and detailed feedback on its progress. This expectation is likely to be stronger when the other professional has, in effect, bought in the service. The counsellor's perspective on this will be different, being based on the premise that only the client sets the agenda for the work. Detailed feedback, either verbally or through making available case notes, would be a breach of confidentiality. Where a third party is involved in setting up a counselling contract for a young person, it is vital that these issues are clarified before embarking on the work. Failure to do so pollutes the counselling process, causes misunderstanding and creates unrealistic expectations on the part of the referring professional. Effective liaison, good communications and possibly staff training about the counselling process is needed so that other workers understand the counsellor's perspective and appreciate the nature of the work.

The issue of inappropriate requests for information is exemplified by the following case. A counsellor working in an agency was asked by a general practitioner for an assessment of the emotional state of a bulimic client who was claiming benefit as she was unable to work. The client was a very private person and certainly did not wish anything she had shared with the counsellor to be revealed, or any assessment of her state to be made or recorded. The counsellor had no choice but to respect her wishes and refuse the doctor's request. The doctor responded with a very angry letter accusing the counsellor of being uncooperative and unhelpful. It was therefore necessary for the director of this particular project to meet the doctor and try and put forward the counsellor's case. At first she was met with hostility and anger but by acknowledging the doctor's feelings and sympathizing with his difficulty she was able to diffuse the situation to the point where the doctor was willing to listen to her argument and understand. He became a great friend of the agency and a constant source of referral.

CONFIDENTIALITY

Confidentiality is always seen by counsellors as a prerequisite for the client–counsellor relationship. However confidentiality is rarely absolute. In supervision for example, even when the client is presented anonymously, the confidentiality is extended to include a third party. Training courses and the use of case studies means that students, who are often the mainstay of counselling agencies, will not be keeping absolute confidentiality within the confines of the agency. These changes in thinking have been reflected in the BAC *Code of Ethics and Practice*. The code now, while emphasizing the importance of confidentiality, also outlines the importance of telling the client the limits to the level of confidentiality offered:

> Confidentiality is a means of providing the client with safety and privacy. For this reason any limitation on the degree of confidentiality offered is likely to diminish the usefulness of counselling.

> (BAC 1992)

The code then goes on to state:

> Counsellors should take all reasonable steps to communicate clearly the extent of confidentiality they are offering to clients.

This should normally be made clear in the pre-counselling information or initial contracting.
If counsellors include consultations with colleagues and others within the confidential relationship, this should be stated to the client at the beginning of counselling.

(BAC 1992)

Clearly the counsellor must take responsibility for involving the client in the contract of confidentiality. It is therefore essential for counsellors to be aware of the level of confidentiality within the school or agency. This will depend on factors such as the type of service offered, issues of child protection, the age of the young person, and for voluntary agencies, funding.

Before we look at this further it is useful to consider the legal aspects of confidentiality and young people. In recent years there has been a tendency to give young people more rights in the area of confidentiality. The Gillick decision of 1985 supported the doctor's right to make a clinical decision to give contraceptive advice without parental knowledge or consent to young people under the age of 16, if they were unwilling to have their parents involved. However the doctor had to ensure that the person was mature enough to understand the consequences and ramifications of their actions. This resulted in a move away from absolute parental authority to an acknowledgement of the increased rights and responsibilities of young people when they have sufficient understanding and intelligence to give informed consent. This concept is referred to as a 'Gillick competent child'. In practice this has meant that parents do not need to be consulted before contraceptive advice or treatment is given, as long as the young person has sufficient understanding and intelligence. Similarly young people requiring counselling, who have sufficient understanding and intelligence, do not have to consult their parents, nor does the counsellor have to inform their parents that counselling has taken place.

The Children Act 1989 also accepts the principle of the 'Gillick competent child' but does not further clarify the rights of children with regard to confidentiality and counselling. It does recommend inter-agency co-operation in cases of child abuse, but unfortunately does not consider that the ethical implications of shared information between agencies could be in direct opposition to a young person's request for confidential counselling: a concern which has been voiced by the Children's Legal Centre. There is clearly an important area of concern arising from this, relating to how the

Children Act affects the counsellor working with young people within a school or voluntary agency.

The age and maturity of the child will have a bearing on the level of understanding and intelligence required to assess whether the young person is 'Gillick competent' and therefore able to understand the problem they want help with, separate from parental involvement. An exception to this would be if the child was being abused by the parent or guardian or when the child is in immediate physical danger even though they were considered to be a 'Gillick competent child'. However, in these cases there would also be the issue of child protection and the possible necessity of involving statutory agencies.

Section 47 of the Children Act places a duty on local authorities to investigate situations where the child could be suffering significant harm. Social Service departments carry out this duty, but counsellors working in any organization bound by these local authority rules are expected to liaise with Social Services and provide relevant information and advice. Guidelines relating to this are issued in some local authorities, but there is a great deal of diversity in the amount of co-operation expected, and at what point this should occur. The Children Act is specific in requiring relevant information to be contributed by anyone working with a young person during an 'enquiry', but it appears some counsellors have been expected to pass on information to Social Services as a matter of course, whether or not an enquiry is under way. This is in fact beyond the statutory requirements of the Act, although inter-agency co-operation is, as we have seen, encouraged by the Act. Professional judgement concerning when to disclose alleged abuse can be used, as even a strict interpretation of the law only requires communication to social services *when requested.* As Bond argues:

> Counsellors working in the specified agencies may be able to use the law to argue against any automatic communication of information to social services, which is only required 'if called upon by the authority to do so' (S.47(9)). It seems reasonable to assume that an Act which has taken into account a Law Commission and extensive consultation at many stages would have imposed a general duty on these specified agencies to take the initiative in the communication of information about abuse if this is what was intended. Instead, the Act avoids creating this general duty.
>
> (Bond 1993: 136)

Schools and agencies will usually have a written policy on confidentiality. If not, they would be well advised to. In some schools the head teacher is informed of cases of abuse, in others a nominated member of staff is responsible for the child protection issues. They liaise closely with Social Services, and other members of staff can discuss child protection issues with them in the first instance.

Young people's information and counselling agencies differ in their level of confidentiality depending on factors such as the structure of the management committee and their source of funding. It can be that management committee members, who may be representative of other statutory bodies, are particularly concerned that the agency offers high levels of confidentiality which are not available in their own setting. Some voluntary agencies have very high levels of confidentiality, particularly those not funded by statutory bodies. In these agencies, even with cases of abuse, Social Services would only be contacted if the client specifically requested this. However, as both counsellors, and the agencies which employ them, wish first and foremost to offer the best possible service to the young person and work for their benefit, the emphasis would be on working towards an outcome which would protect the client and stop the abuse.

Where agencies are funded by Social Services, youth and community or health departments, it is important to have very specific guidelines on how to proceed in cases of abuse or suspected abuse of young people under the age of 18. Many authorities will have their own guidelines for teachers and youth and health workers, but these may not be sensitive to, or recognize sufficiently, the confidential nature of the counselling relationship. Some require immediate reporting of all cases of suspected abuse so that Social Services can decide whether or not to investigate. If clear guidelines are provided, counsellors and other volunteers will be able to follow a set of procedures. In our opinion, these should include:

1 Clear direction relating to when consultation should take place with a supervisor and/or the co-ordinator of the service in order to decide the best way to proceed.
2 If the young person is at risk, the original contract should be reviewed and if necessary renegotiated with a view to the client retaining as much autonomy as possible in the circumstances.
3 If confidentiality is to be breached, this should be discussed and if possible agreed with the young person. In circumstances where this is not possible and the young person is assessed as a 'Gillick competent child', the implications of such a move should be carefully thought out with regard to that young person and their future relationship with the agency.

In our experience, confidentiality can usually be satisfactorily renegotiated with a young person if there is time and if a good relationship has been built with the child protection team. This means that the counsellor will understand how the matter will proceed with Social Services and how they can offer continuing support to the client. It is particularly useful to have a named contact person in Social Services whose field is child protection, so the agency or individual counsellor can discuss anonymously the outline of the case before any decision to proceed is taken further. Training in this area is essential so that all counsellors follow fully the guidelines and procedures. Otherwise decisions can be made without due consideration and consultation. As Bond suggests:

> I am sure that all counsellors would prefer to prevent abuse whenever possible; however, it seems to me that this ethical intention needs to be balanced by recognition that children of sufficient understanding also need access to a confidential service in which they retain a substantial degree of control over the direct actions taken on their behalf. To offer a child or young person confidential counselling and then routinely to break that confidence, even in response to something as serious as child abuse, is in itself a betrayal of trust and a form of abuse.
>
> (Bond 1993: 137)

Young people need to understand the options open to them and have a clear idea of what will happen if they proceed with disclosure. The counsellor needs to be separate from the actual proceedings which can be handled by the co-ordinator. In this way the counsellor continues to work with and support the young person throughout the process.

Social workers themselves have varying knowledge of counselling. Some will respect the intimate nature of the counselling relationship and are quite happy to discuss ways of working with the young person in order to decide whether or not to proceed with an enquiry. Unfortunately there are still some who wish to take the whole thing out of the agency's hands, and will not discuss anything until they have the name and address of the young person. This lack of trust is becoming less common, probably because of the intervention of child protection teams.

FUNDING

Funding is of great significance to voluntary agencies. It also raises issues with other workers and colleagues. This is particularly so in schools where resources may be scarce and the nature of counselling is not always appreciated by other members of staff. Counselling is both time- and labour-intensive, and when it also demands jostling for scarce funding, it can lead the lone school counsellor to feel exposed and vulnerable. As budgetary responsibility has been devolved from local authorities to individual schools, counselling has to compete with the departmental budgets, libraries and even the running and repair costs. Departmental heads have had to learn to be assertive and demanding to secure and increase their own budgets and staffing levels. In this climate counselling can easily be marginalized and cut.

Another difficulty relating to funding is the increasing expectations of the funders in controlling how money is spent. Applying for funding is in itself a diplomatic minefield, whereby the agency desperately attempts to fit its work to the type of funding available. This is not the end of the story or the difficulties because once funding has been secured, other obligations follow. For instance, a relatively minor request could be that the agency display a funder's logo on all printed material. However, other expectations occur that raise serious ethical issues for the agency, for example being asked to prioritize one group of clients above another. Occasionally funding is secured from a company which is then criticized for political involvement, environmental or health issues and this reflects detrimentally on the agency and potentially alienates possible service users.

RELATIONSHIPS WITHIN THE AGENCY

Many agencies that offer young people counselling also fulfil other roles, including advice work. Counsellors may be seen, or see themselves, as having greater levels of expertise and therefore a higher status than advice workers. This may accurately reflect the clearer routes for counselling training than for advice and information work. In fact both types of work require similar levels of expertise and knowledge. Conflicts arise when one group of workers feel undervalued as this is likely to demotivate them and encourage professional jealousy. Hopefully National Vocational Qualifications (NVQs) will help to improve this situation and the status of advice work, but in the meantime it is important that all members of the agency feel valued in the work they do, and the skills they offer.

There is increasingly a greater recognition that those who run voluntary agencies need good management skills. Any agency where large numbers of volunteer staff do the majority of the face-to-face work needs to be supported and managed by an efficient administrative system. The converse is often the reality, with only one or two part-time workers to carry out most of the management, administration and support within the agency. In many cases they have not been employed for their management skill, but for their knowledge of young people, or previous work as a counsellor or advice worker. At worst this can lead to inappropriate use of resources (including staff who become disenchanted and leave), bad practice (in such matters as health and safety, equal opportunities and child protection issues), and a lack of any proper monitoring of the service. In such circumstances both staff and service users are at risk.

As funding becomes more difficult and accountability essential, efficient management will be paramount to ensure the best use of the resources available. This in itself causes another set of difficulties because workers within the agency do not always adjust well to change. Greater efficiency, quality assurance, and accountability all threaten the more easygoing modes of working that were previously regarded as good enough. Thus tensions can arise between management and staff which need to be handled sensitively, especially when the majority of the work-force is giving its time freely and has a great deal of emotional energy invested in the agency.

The management committee plays a very important part in the life of the agency. A good treasurer is vital, in order to ensure that funds are managed well and that the co-ordinator has a clear idea of available monies and adequate access to them. Someone interested in fund-raising is most definitely an asset, but as this job is very time-consuming few people are willing to volunteer. The committee itself can be very supportive to both the paid workers and volunteers and can help with any difficulties arising from these two groups. However, occasionally there can be opposing views within the management committee itself, or between them and the actual workers, which can make relationships far from easy.

CONCLUSION

In this chapter we have explored the various difficulties that can arise in relations between counsellors and other professionals and within agencies. Issues such as funding, confidentiality and child protection all need to be addressed between counsellors and their colleagues in other professions so that they are all working together to provide the best standard of service to young people. Unfortunately the political climate which promotes the ethics of the marketplace and encourages competition, even when it is completely inappropriate, adds to the difficulties inherent in working together. It can set one group of workers against another to the detriment of all concerned, not least the clients. Nevertheless, there is a great deal of good will and desire to understand and complement each other's work, which needs to be tapped so that the services to young people can be improved instead of eroded.

· SIX ·

A critique of counselling for young people

YOUTH AND COMMUNITY DEPARTMENTS AND VOLUNTARY AGENCIES

We have seen that many of the services provided for young people are from voluntary agencies, whose major funders are county councils, Youth and Community, Social or Health Services and, in some cases, a specific charitable trust. These agencies provide varying degrees of counselling, as one of a variety of services on offer to young people. Young people's needs are diverse and complex and are most appropriately met by specialized services, available on one site. Such centres are set up to be attractive to young people, possibly staffed by them and catering specifically for them. This type of service offers informal counselling on a drop-in basis, as well as formal counselling by appointment by trained volunteers. These are likely to have received their training from within the agency and would most likely be using a person-centred model.

Other services offer only formal counselling, often recruiting from Diploma in Counselling courses and initially providing student placements to attract volunteers. As these centres are likely to recruit from a number of courses, a variety of theoretical orientations will be represented, each counsellor working within his or her framework, but in accordance with the ethos of the agency.

Either of these approaches have a great deal to offer young people. The commitment of volunteers is usually very high and a great deal of good work is accomplished. However as money becomes increasingly constrained, many of these services are facing cutbacks and some are closing altogether. This is very regrettable as services to young people in the voluntary sector are highly cost-effective. In reality they often run on a few thousand pounds which pays for telephones, heating, lighting, stationery, publicity and volunteer expenses. The other two major costs are a co-ordinator and premises.

In the last few years there has been a greater recognition of the need for counselling in all spheres of work and community provision. This is also true of youth counselling. Youth and community departments in some areas have begun to develop county-wide schemes of Youth Enquiry Services (YES) which usually include a component of counselling. Some of these are loosely based upon the National Youth Agency (NYA) initiative of the National Youth Bureau mentioned in Chapter 1, but with no comparable funding.

Some counties like Hampshire, Berkshire and, more recently, Buckinghamshire and Hertfordshire, have begun to co-ordinate the services that are available through each borough. Inevitably the level of co-ordination varies. For example, Hampshire has a well-developed service at Havant and Portsmouth, Off the Record and Open Door in Aldershot, as well as a network of other young people's counselling and information services, for example Just Us, No Limits, Moving On Project and It's Your Choice. All these agencies have different funding bodies. Since 1993, directors and co-ordinators of these agencies have begun to meet monthly to devise common policies with regard to issues such as training volunteers, confidentiality, and training programmes for supervisors.

Similarly in Hertfordshire, Youth and Community Services have appointed four co-ordinators to cover the four sections of the county with a brief to set up services in all the major areas. Initially each area was allocated a few thousand pounds for revenue, but each co-ordinator is expected to develop agencies in partnership with other interested parties, so funding can be raised and shared. Each initiative is expected in the long-term to become self-financing. This is quite a major task at a time when any funding is hard to negotiate, but especially so when money is needed for ongoing but essential expenses, for instance renting premises. As in Hampshire the co-ordinators recognize the need to develop county-wide policies which can then be adopted by those interested in developing counselling and information services in their part of the county. Centralized policies ensure the existence of guidelines for good practice that can be adopted by the various groups. These guidelines will cover core issues, for example, how to recruit volunteer counsellors and information workers, confidentiality, minimum requirements for location, and resources. In this way a cohesive framework and standards of practice are developed with the aim of ensuring a high-quality service. Eventually this will result in joint training initiatives and service provision across the county. This will take time but it is hoped that a common policy will prevent new agencies from continually reinventing the wheel and will enable useful and productive sharing of practice.

Berkshire is one of the larger county services where an example of good practice that is worth examining, 'No 5', is based in Reading. This agency was established in 1970 and is now a registered charity. It originally developed as a direct response to the needs of young people in Reading. Although a voluntary agency in its own right, it also enjoys a close relationship with the Royal County of Berkshire Youth and Community Service and is one of the largest services in the country and the major agency in Berkshire. The Royal County of Berkshire and Reading Borough Council are its major funders. The mission statement for 'No 5' states: 'No 5 exists so that young people and others can enjoy the benefits of a free confidential and professional Counselling and Information service and thereby be empowered to lead full lives.'

Currently it has 120 personnel, most of whom are volunteers. Apart from counselling and information, it also offers specialized groups such as 'Tranx', 'Self Harm' and 'Food Relationships'.

One of the remits of No 5 is to liaise and work collaboratively with its sister agencies, SPACE, No 22, NYCAS (Newbury Youth Counselling and Advisory Service), Youthline, and Listening Spot. This is an important part of the work of No 5 as it is these links which enable the service to have a county perspective, although each agency is self-governing. There is an agency in each of Berkshire's six districts, catering for the multi-faceted needs of young people. However they are all funded, managed, staffed and operated differently. This reflects the inevitable variation in the needs of young people in each specific area. For example, SPACE in Slough caters for the needs of many Asian young people. The one common denominator among these agencies is training. Anyone who wishes to work as a counsellor must undertake the training run by No 5, which is organized and funded in conjunction with Berkshire Youth and Community Service. At present this is a 92-hour course, soon to be increased to 150 hours. The course is accredited by the University of Oxford Delegacy of Local Examinations, and successful completion leads to a Certificate in Professional Studies. For those who wish to continue studying, the Diploma in Professional Studies is a further 150 hours of training. All the training is based on a credit scheme whereby the student accrues credits through study and experiential work until they have the required number for accreditation. This is not unlike the new NVQ system discussed later in this chapter.

Apart from common training for counsellors, all the trainers are recruited from people who have at least two years experience in the service and have completed the 'Training the Trainer' course. Other than this there is surprisingly little else these six services have as common policy. Co-ordinators meet every six to eight weeks to discuss elements of training but there is no common policy on management structure, practice and issues pertaining to agency philosophy, for example confidentiality. County policies govern recruitment and selection, but there is agency diversity on what is incorporated. Most services select aspects relevant to their particular remit of work, and as each is an autonomous agency with charitable funding in its own right, it has the freedom to do this in dialogue with its management committee.

So although in one sense a county-wide service, the reality is the agencies are a group of six very separate organizations without common policy, but all benefiting from Youth and Community Services involvement, primarily through the well-established training programmes for potential counsellors and youth workers alike. The advantage of this structure is the autonomy of these agencies. However, on the minus side, most are underfunded and understaffed. This makes it difficult to find the time to make and implement the policies and agency philosophy that are arguably an essential corner-stone to good practice.

One might imagine that a county-wide service, promoted by the Youth Service, would have an underlying philosophy and common policy that has been considered and produced by existing agencies sharing their experience. Recommendations could then be considered by all and implemented, as an agreed initiative, by old and newly formed agencies. However this is rarely the case. One way forward for youth counselling is through initiatives similar to those found in Berkshire that could be adopted by other counties. Alternatively other counties could develop their own policies, with existing agencies, to produce guidelines that would share expertise and good practice and be a useful resource to new projects.

In September 1994, Youth Access released a draft copy of its *Code of Ethics and Practice*. The standards laid out in this code 'seek to establish a common frame of reference by which agencies will manage their services'. It states that the purpose of the code is to provide a framework based on the *BAC Code of Ethics and Practice* but which would be applicable 'across youth information, advice, and counselling services . . . recognising the breadth and depth of the work of the agencies' (1994: 1). The code is an excellent document which sets out the value base central to the work, which is to be person-centred, non-judgemental, anti-oppressive and non-discriminatory.

The code states that the agency is responsible for ensuring the workers are 'competent to perform the range and depth of duties offered by the agency' and that the agency 'provide[s] staff development, monitoring and evaluation of the service' (1994: 2). The code of practice also requires each agency to formulate policies on issues such as confidentiality, contracting, supervision, disciplinary and grievance procedures.

We have seen that funding is one of the most important issues for every youth counselling service. An interesting project which has been able to develop as a result of sound funding is Mancroft Advice in Norwich. It is also a good example of an agency which has been developed through consultation with young people and has developed services as a direct response to their expressed needs.

MANCROFT ADVICE

This agency provides information, advice, counselling and a whole range of other services, which have been initiated and developed by young people, with help from youth workers. It began in 1991 after a survey of young people on the streets highlighted the need for a drop-in provision, offering a safe environment, and information and advice services that would be aimed specifically at young people. Counselling was also seen as an important resource, with emphasis on providing it in a way that would suit young people. Many of those had already experienced counselling in, for example, drug and alcohol agencies but these were often experienced as not catering for their needs, being staffed by counsellors not in tune with young people.

The project consists of a drop-in coffee bar and a large information and advice room with telephones that can be used for accommodation and job enquiries. There are also two counselling rooms, a kitchen and an office. Seven counsellors have been carefully selected for both their expertise in counselling and their experience with young people. One works with couples and the other six on an individual basis and all are paid, a rare occurrence in young people's agencies! Individual supervision is also provided. On average 40 clients are seen a week.

In addition, there are three to four unpaid advice workers, and part-time youth workers run the coffee bar. All users are actively involved, through attending a monthly meeting, when issues about the running of the centre, its facilities and general appearance are discussed. As a result of these meetings nappy-changing facilities have been introduced and courses run, such as first aid. New initiatives have been developed, for instance, a young fathers' group has been started to complement the existing young mothers' group. The latter meets twice a week to provide continuing education and formal qualifications for young mothers who can no longer attend school. A doctor and a careers adviser are also available, as well as a free pregnancy testing service.

Another interesting development is a monthly listings magazine of the arts, called *Big City, Bright Lights*, which covers the music, cinema, and theatre scene in Norwich. This is put together and printed in the centre and sold in the town. There is also a gay and lesbian magazine called *Shout* which is similarly produced. Little outreach work is required as the centre is well known in the town and knowledge of its facilities, including the counselling service, is passed on by word of mouth.

The major funder is the Riseborough Trust which sponsors the project through an educational charity administered from the Peter Mancroft Church in the centre of Norwich. Some money is provided and part-time posts paid for from the Youth and Community budget. This supports the youth workers who run the coffee bar and who also offer informal counselling and befriending to those not wanting formal counselling.

We see this as an excellent example of a project which involves young people in a meaningful way in the running of the centre, is able to respond to the changing needs of its users, and offers a variety of services which cater to the different types of young people in Norwich. Compared to most services it is extremely well funded and, more importantly, funded consistently. Unlike so many agencies, it is not forced to annually review services in terms of making cuts because budgets are being reduced or axed. It does not exist on the knife edge, wondering whether it will survive another year.

Share in Taunton is a good but sad example of a project which is facing closure as a result of withdrawal of funding. At present it receives funding from the Health Service for working in the drugs field. However, the local authority has rethought its strategy and wants to reorganize and offer help to *all* ages in the drug field. Hence it has withdrawn its money. As a result another funder, the National Children's Home (NCH), along with Social Services and the Youth Service, will withdraw its funding which is conditional on the level of funding received from other organizations. With the imbalance caused by the Health Service withdrawal, coupled with the NCH's own policy of moving toward more family-based work,

Share will be forced to close in March 1995. It hopes to reopen in April if it has been successful in negotiating new funding from other sources.

Money for counselling may continue to be available through Department of Health grants. Specific projects like HIV and AIDS, and other areas of sexual health will probably still attract funding, particularly under 'The Health of the Nation' scheme, but less specific types of counselling could be under threat. An example of a joint mental health and youth and community project is one that was set up in Letchworth in Hertfordshire. A part-time counsellor was appointed to counsel young people who might otherwise become 'labelled' as a result of coming into contact with psychiatric services. What they needed was short-term counselling. Young people using the services of the mental health team were assessed and if it seemed that the most appropriate intervention was counselling, they were offered a short-term contract with this specially employed counsellor. Unfortunately the project was only funded for three years and as the post-holder has left it seems unlikely she will be replaced.

At present the future does not look particularly bright for the field of youth counselling. The Youth Service's recent interest in the areas of information, advice and counselling rather than centre-based work looked hopeful, but as youth and community departments themselves are having their funding cut or being disbanded, the picture is not reassuring. Possibly the Youth Service will continue to support some aspects of the work, such as information and advice, which frequently has a higher profile than counselling. There is often an expectation that it is cheaper, only requiring some basic information packs and some enthusiastic volunteers. In fact this is certainly not the case: information work, like counselling, requires a great deal of training in both accessing material and in delivery. A good deal of sensitivity on the part of the volunteer is necessary if the work is to be carried out effectively. Unlike counselling there are no courses to become qualified in the field unless a person has already undergone training in an organization like the Citizens Advice Bureau. Hopefully the advent of NVQs will rectify this situation.

NEW PROJECTS FOR BLACK AND ASIAN YOUNG PEOPLE

The way forward in counselling for black and Asian young people is in our opinion, through providing services staffed by members of, and based in these communities. Mainstream counselling in Britain is Eurocentric and as such can be perceived as having very little to do with the lives of non-white British young people. Worse still, it may be seen as posing a threat to the communities themselves and to the family life that is so central to them. Services which are community-based are likely to be better received, supported and funded. Staff working in such agencies will have a cultural perspective matching that of the community, and the day-to-day experience of living with racism. In the three such projects we will describe, staff have a mainstream counselling training as well as community-based staffing and location. This ensures both their competence and their value to the wider community in terms of their training role.

The Time Out project

The Caribbean Women's Association, which is based in the Lozells district of Birmingham, is responsible for setting up an interesting new project called 'Time Out', which aims to provide counselling from an Afrocentric perspective to young black people in its area. Its target age range is 6 to 21 years of age with flexibility as appropriate. At present it has five counsellors, all Afro-Caribbean women and all qualified to at least diploma level. Each counsellor sees three clients a week. Staff operate a waiting list system. Supervision is at present provided on a six-weekly basis. Time Out is partly funded by Birmingham Social Services department, and the service is offered free of charge, although users may contribute if they so wish. Clients are self-referring or come to the service via other agencies, for example, Social Services.

Time Out's primary objective is clearly stated as 'empowerment and personal development for individuals'. Its approach is impressive in its clarity and in its expectation of the mutual respect which seems to underpin the work. Users of the service are given clear information and guidelines about their rights and responsibilities and a code of conduct. The document is neither apologetic nor patronizing and young people coming to counselling for the first time would soon understand what they can expect and what would be expected of them in terms of behaviour, keeping to the contract and non-discriminatory practice. The document reads as follows:

USER'S RIGHTS
As a user of the 'Time Out' service, you have the right to;

1 Be informed of the nature of the service being offered and what it aims to do before deciding whether you wish to use it.

2 Be informed of when the service is available and for how long.
3 Be informed of i) any records that are kept.
                     ii) who sees them and how secure they are.
                    iii) the reasons for keeping them and your right of access to them.
4 To withhold your name and address. A postcode is enough for information needed by funders. However, it is important to have a telephone number or address where you can be contacted in case we need to cancel an appointment.
5 Be informed of the confidentiality of the service. However, if a disclosure of physical/sexual abuse is made we have the legal duty to report this to the Social Services department.
6 Be consulted and your permission gained before any information that you have shared with the counsellor goes outside your relationship. You will be informed who will be told and the reason for this.
7 Review on a regular basis the counselling situation that you are in.
8 Complain if you are unhappy with the service.

The Caribbean Women's Association believes that young people, as any other service user have the right to:

• Express themselves
• Be responsible for their actions
• Make informed choices
• Be respected
• Be heard
• Be taken seriously.

USER'S RESPONSIBILITIES
As a user of 'Time Out', you are responsible for:

1 Keeping appointments when made and calling to cancel, giving 24 hours notice if you are unable to attend.
2 Being mindful of yourself and your conduct towards others.
3 Respecting every service user who comes into contact with the service i.e. other users, counsellors, project workers or management committee members and members of the organization.
4 Punctuality – any lateness will be deducted from your counselling session.
5 Respecting the no-smoking policy of the building.
6 Completing an evaluation sheet after each six-week period.

Counselling is offered for drug and alcohol abuse, bereavement, physical, sexual or verbal abuse, identity crisis and any other issue. What is important is that this service is being offered to black young people by black women who share not only the cultural background but also the experience of racism and its survival and who in themselves provide a very positive role model.

The Time Out project is part of a much wider service being offered to the community by the Caribbean Women's Association, who provide social and cultural support to black people in their area. They have a Children in Care Project which not only provides anti-oppressive practice training to care workers and foster parents working with black children but also works with the children and their carers on identity awareness issues, hair and skin care and Caribbean cuisine. They have exciting plans for the future too. They aim to start a youth project for 12- to 18-year-olds, a playgroup and day nursery, a latch key service, an elderly drop-in centre, a cultural library and a meals on wheels service providing Caribbean food.

The Black Therapy Centre

The Black Therapy Centre was conceived in 1991 during a conference on 'Black Therapy' held in Birmingham. One of the issues addressed was the sheer lack in numbers of black counsellors and fewer black psychotherapists. Many felt isolated in their work and enjoyed the opportunity of sharing practice and discussing ideological concerns. As a result, in 1993 the centre was opened in Ealing. One purpose is to provide a place where information, training and other resources are available as well as a place to discuss models of black therapy practice and offer ongoing therapy.

The therapeutic services are not age-specific, and were motivated by the paucity of service available to black people. The centre is 'owned' by income raised by the black community through fees for therapy, if the person can afford to pay, and donations. The local council and health authority have offered funding but this has been turned down as the idea of black community ownership is central to the centre. Young people would not be expected to pay but it is very likely their parents would. This is discussed with the parents, so that it does not impinge on the therapy itself. The centre believes in supporting the whole family so separate therapy can be offered to parents.

In working with young black people the Black Therapy Centre attempts to fulfil two central goals: self-knowledge on internal, social, historical, physical, political and spiritual levels; and broadening of perception of themselves as a young black man or woman. This is done by various means, some recognizable as traditional (Western) therapy. Other methods, for example Black History classes, training in drumming, dance and African herbalism may be deemed outside the remit of counselling or therapy. The Black Therapy model is philosophically based on Kawaida theory (Karenga: 1980), which brings together common themes in the philosophy of people of colour throughout the world. This philosophy has been made into a model of therapy, defined and refined in practice by Francis and Ali (1993).

In working individually with young black people, a time-limited frame of 12 weeks is used, after which clients are moved into an open black identity-awareness group for up to two years. The group is based on a theoretical understanding of black identity as outlined by Cross (1980) and piloted and developed by Bailey and Phillips (1990).

During this time, four therapy weekends are offered annually on 'Transitions to Adulthood'. These are three-day intensive therapy experiences where a group of up to 12 young people explore their past roles and responsibilities as children and their new roles of responsibilities as men and women with a facilitated series of exercises, tasks and shared experiences. This is done through a modern initiation ceremony informed by the thoughts, personal experience and work of Malidoma Some and the theories of Julia and Nathan Hare (1985).

Most referrals come directly from the black community through advertisements in the black media or, importantly, through word of mouth. Some of the referrals come from the local health authority and Social Services although these are not given priority.

This is a unique and innovative project that sees young people within a holistic context. This allows the family to be supported as well as the young person, and deals directly with the issues of black identity faced by young black people. It also offers a culturally relevant model of work based on the growing literature, at present predominantly from the United States. However one of the priorities of the centre is to bring together such material and make it accessible to the black community, as well as generating its own. It can also provide organizations nationally with a network of contacts if difficulty is experienced finding black therapists.

The Yakeen project

This project aims to be operational by 1995 and originates from an Asian women's organization in the Harrow area known as DAWN

(Deep Asian Women's Network). The project aims to provide a counselling service for young Asian women, between the approximate ages of 15 and 30. It grew from concern about the high rate of suicide nationally among young Asian women.

'Yakeen' means 'to trust' and it is a word which bridges many of the languages of the Indian subcontinent. It is hoped that it will be understood by the target client group. The choice of title is significant. It is the intention of the founders that the service will be trusted by its clients, through the establishment of good practice with regard to confidentiality and boundaries. It also aims to be trusted by the community who, it is hoped, will come to see the service as complementing the well-established family and community networks.

Yakeen is to be funded by Harrow Social Services out of their mental health budget. The building is self-contained and on two floors, with a reception and information area on the ground floor and counselling rooms upstairs. As well as counselling it hopes to offer advice, support and some group work, including self-help groups. The staff group will consist of a co-ordinator, one full-time counsellor and one sessional counsellor; in the future it is planned to take volunteer counsellors who are likely to be diploma students.

The job description for the co-ordinator asks for a background in social work or similar field, a diploma in counselling, experience of working within the Asian community and fluency in at least one Asian language. The standards set are high, reflecting the desire to establish a high-quality service. Managerial supervision will be in-house but there will be provision for external non-managerial supervision.

As far was possible, care will·be taken to ensure that clients are assigned to counsellors who are not known to their families; this attention to boundaries will extend to supervision. Referrals will come through GPs, hospitals, colleges, Social Services and through self-referral. The project plans to advertise itself through the existing community networks, the Asian press, radio and television.

The founders of the project recognize they are offering a service to young women only and that this leaves a large gap in the overall provision. They are keen not to be seen as anti-men or as presenting any kind of challenge to Asian family life. They know that they will have to work hard to be seen as supportive to the family and to Asian ways of life. What is impressive about this project is the high standards of practice that are being established from the outset. They do not intend to reinvent the wheel but will draw on the experience of other projects, use BAC's code of ethics, creating a service of real value to their community. At present they are fortunate in

having their funding on a fairly sound basis, which makes these
aspirations possible. Long may it continue.

NYA AND THE INFORMATION SHOP

Over the last twenty years, both the statutory and voluntary sides
of the Youth Service have established a growing number of young
people's information centres. The NYA has sought to provide an
information specification to outline the necessary facilities that are
in line with its Information Shop initiative (formerly the Youth
Bureau's). As the introduction to the specification states:

> The NYA is also the major impetus behind the Information
> Shop initiative, which will offer high quality high-street in-
> formation provision to young people, and, through its trading
> company Under 26 Ltd, has launched a youth card which will
> entitle under 26 year olds to discounts on a range of goods
> and services in the UK and 15 other countries.
>
> (McDonald 1990: 1)

The specification booklet outlines the range of services which will
be provided and 'specifies the factors which will contribute to a
high quality provision' (McDonald 1990: 7). It clearly proposes the
aims and objectives, and states the principles of youth information
provision. Target groups are defined: it suggests the locations which
should be 'high profile' and 'popular with young people', and advocates a corporate identity and common logo. How the shop will
function is described, and how the service will be delivered and
staffed. The management process is also discussed, as is monitoring
and evaluating provision, and the role of the central unit. Appendices cover the types of topics requested by young people and examines what is good practice in recruitment and selection procedure.

Running costs for one year exclusive of rent and rates are estimated as being £128,700, including a co-ordinator and two full-
time information workers, an administrative assistant and some
part-time hours for outreach work. In comparison an average counselling and information agency such as Signpost in Watford costs
approximately £44,000 per year including staffing and revenue.
Signpost relies heavily on volunteers to reduce costs, reflecting the
difficulty in today's climate of securing adequate funding. It might
be assumed that the NYA has estimated the annual running costs
as an ideal, although it is difficult to imagine how many of the
other specifications can be carried out unless there is a core of paid

staff which represents the largest proportion of the cost. However, as Peter White states in *Information Shops in Action*:

> Strict adherence to the specification is unpopular, and can seem pedantic and bureaucratic during the excitement of planning a much needed project for young people. But it is vital – and achievable, as the growing list of successful Shops testify.
>
> (White 1993: 51)

and later:

> Information Shops only work if they are devised the hard way, from the bottom up, and based on extensive knowledge of local need and character. But they cannot open piecemeal, dipping a tentative toe in the water to see what works – the stringent requirements of the national specification rule this out.
>
> (White 1993: 54)

In the summer of 1993, eight Information Shops were in operation: in Bradford, Halton, Horsham, Accrington, Ilkley, Mansfield, Nottingham, and Rochester. Further shops are developing in Gloucester, Greenwich, Rochdale and Sheffield. Compared to this, 45 new counselling and information services were listed in the Youth Access Directory Supplement covering developments in 1993. (This includes five in Scotland – an area not covered by NYA.) While on the one hand, the Information Shop specification contains much valuable material and youth counselling services could benefit from a more cohesive approach, on the other hand, the specification does tend to be somewhat prescriptive. The large amount of funding required means it is not feasible for small towns without large commercial businesses. Our own recent experience highlights this difficulty: setting up the Dacorum youth counselling service in Hemel Hempstead was done with only £1,000, one part-time worker, an enormous amount of support and enthusiasm from young people and a multitude of agencies. The service is still struggling to get any funding or premises other than those kindly offered to us by the local family centre. This is undoubtedly 'piecemeal and tentative' but cannot be otherwise unless someone funds a worker to raise the level of money the specification requires. Unless there is commitment to youth information and counselling, as shown by the Dutch government and its funding of the JACs (Chapter 1), the long-term prospects of many agencies are poor.

Finally, although the specification mentions counselling, it is not a service Information Shops seek to provide in the formal sense, although they may act as a base for delivery from another source. Some services have recruited qualified counsellors, but generally the Information Shops have no clear guidelines or specifications for this type of work, for example provision for supervision. Rather, counselling is used informally in the process of good information work, and youth workers are called information counsellors. It would be different if, as in The Netherlands, youth counselling was provided in a separate type of agency. However, this is not the case and this may ultimately mean that the only type of counselling provided will be informal. We feel formal counselling is an important service that should be available to young people, particularly in these high profile well-funded and well-supported shops.

CHILD PROTECTION

Inevitably child protection is an important issue when examining counselling provision for young people. The Child Advocacy Service, which has been piloted in Plymouth, is an exciting new development that aims to bridge the gap between what Social Services can offer young people who have been abused and the local Youth Enquiry Service (YES) who are specialised in working with young people.

The idea for this project was conceived by the NSPCC and developed by them, Social Services and the YES. Its aim is to provide advocacy for children of 10 years or over involved in child protection issues. The underlying hypothesis is that children can participate in a meaningful way when they are provided with an independent advocate. This enables them to take part in case conferences so that their views are heard. Volunteers with the necessary skills and understanding were recruited from YES to work in partnership with other agencies. They underwent further training with the NSPCC on legal aspects of child protection, the case conference process and the advocate's role within it. Total confidentiality is the policy of YES with the proviso that anything the advocate is told that is considered life-threatening would be taken to the line managers.

The pilot scheme demonstrated the advantages of the service for both the young person and the professionals involved, the latter benefiting from gaining clarity on the issues involved in each case. Of the 23 children who were referred to the project 80 per cent used the service and participated in the process of child protection

procedures, compared to only 20 per cent in the whole of the West
of England, before the scheme began. It also probably represents
the highest number of children participating in any region of the
country. As the report concludes:

> The project has proved an extremely positive service for both
> the children and others involved in this process. The children
> want and have the right to be involved. Their involvement
> did not adversely effect decision making. In fact plans made
> were often more acceptable to the young person and more
> appropriate to that young person's protection needs. Allowing
> the child to participate has offered them a much greater under-
> standing and as a result some preventative plans were able to
> be implemented avoiding costly and obtrusive intervention.
>   (Stephens and Scutt 1993)

Although this is not counselling, it is an interesting inter-agency
initiative which is to be welcomed by counsellors. As we have seen,
child protection is an unavoidable issue when working with young
people. Counsellors are often wary of the avenues of reporting and
the processes to follow, and are frequently concerned that the system may repeat the abusive pattern. An advocacy service allows
those young people involved to be empowered and enabled to be
heard. This would reassure counsellors, and would be an important
way of bringing agencies together to ease the tension that often
occurs between them. As the advocates are already working in a
young people's service, better links with counsellors could be maintained, thereby resulting in a comprehensive support service for
young people going through these traumatic procedures. As the
report says: 'The overall aim of advocacy is to empower the children
and young people sufficiently to be able to eventually self advocate.' (Stephens and Scutt 1993).

CO-ORDINATORS

In any critique of young people's counselling services it is essential
to examine the role of the co-ordinator or director. This may not be
a full-time post, particularly if the agency is relatively small or new.
Even the large well-funded agencies, like Centre 33, have only two
full-time posts and most manage with one full-time person and
perhaps a part-time worker or two.

The counselling co-ordinator needs considerable skills in managing
the volunteers, who are essential to the agency in terms of seeing

clients and offering them the services available. An agency may have anything from 20 to over 100 volunteers each giving on average three hours a week of their time, excluding supervision and other forms of support. Managing a workforce that is coming in for short periods of time creates problems relating to both organization and personnel. The co-ordinator needs both management expertise and the ability to motivate volunteers and ensure they feel valued and appreciated. Keeping volunteers motivated can be difficult especially when a service is new and few young people are actually using the facilities. Even in well-established services this can be problematic when times are slack, and few young people are phoning or coming through the door.

Most counselling agencies have selection procedures which are both rigorous and demanding. This is particularly important as potential volunteers may be trying to meet their own needs rather than having a real ability there to help young people. Agencies who are not so rigorously selective rely more on sympathetic voluntary helpers: they may find that this can create more difficulties than it solves as unselected volunteers can require more support than potential customers. This of course is not unique to youth agencies, but can be further exacerbated by a transferential relationship between the person holding the manager role, who is perceived/behaves as parent and the volunteer who is perceived/behaves as child, or perhaps more accurately, rebellious adolescent. This can be very difficult for the lone co-ordinator, who can feel very isolated in his or her position, particularly if their role is the only paid post. The very fact of one person being paid for their work, when everyone else is a volunteer, can lead to unrealistic expectations and resentment from volunteers. Co-ordinators can find themselves expected to do every task as well as knowing about each counsellor's clients. Not surprisingly many co-ordinators fall into the trap of trying to be all things to all people. They put in many hours of extra time, feeling indispensable and fearing that no one else can be counted upon to carry out the multitude of tasks. This can, partly at least, reflect reality.

The co-ordinator/director may also be in a delicate position between the volunteers on the one hand, and the management committee on the other. Ideally all are working together and supporting the volunteers to carry out the work with the clients. However, sometimes this is not the case and the co-ordinator becomes the 'piggy in the middle' between these two groups. Coupled with the constant threat of funding being withdrawn or not materializing, this can make the lot of the co-ordinator extremely stressful. It can sound an impossible task and the fact that many people enthusiastically and energetically fulfil this role is a testament to their commitment and motivation.

PERFORMANCE INDICATORS

Youth Access, which is in the forefront in campaigning to give youth counselling a high profile, has recognized the importance of maintaining funding. It has tried to address the needs of its members by producing a booklet on performance indicators called *A Measure of Good Practice* (Thomson: 1993). It aims to produce a model that can be adapted locally to measure the performance targets set by any agency. It recognizes supervision as part of the evaluation process, and also includes statistical analysis in the interpretation of performance. Six points are put forward for every agency to consider:

* The need for a statement of purpose;
* The need to agree and understand the value base;
* The political and social context of the organization;
* Agree to collect only the data which will be useful;
* The value of corporate commitment;
* The role of professional judgement – evaluation is based on the purpose for which the service exists.

(Thomson 1993: 11)

This is a useful resource for all youth information, advice and counselling services as it is written specifically for that type of work. As previously discussed in Chapter 3, it also recognizes the need for user/client feedback in the ongoing evaluation of each project:

> Projects need to monitor and evaluate their usage and constantly evidence the needs of young people, and the relevance of the services provided. To achieve this the agencies should justify their existence and the impact they have on young people. Evaluation helps service development through systematic monitoring of the needs of the young people in their own communities.

(Thomson 1993: 24)

RESEARCH

There is little research in the field of youth counselling, doubtless again reflecting the problem of funding. As has been stressed throughout this book this is the greatest difficulty faced by any youth counselling service. Without this, services are inevitably destined to be inadequate and competent research will fall by the wayside. Thus although Youth Access is the body that supports and publicizes all services providing counselling for young people, unfortunately it does not have the time or the resources to be actively involved in research. However it does act as an invaluable source of communication between youth counselling services through its annual training days and twice-yearly co-ordinators events. This facilitates the sharing of ideas, issues, and difficulties both workers and co-ordinators experience in this field.

Some co-ordinators who have been studying for higher degrees have undertaken interesting although small-scale research projects. For example, Kevin Feaviour from Off The Record has explored the attitudes of clients and providers of youth counselling services in relation to four areas: confidentiality, informality of service provision, specificity in offering services particularly for young people and independence of the agency from other organizations. After examining the relevant literature on the subject, he concluded:

> One area, however, seems to be missing – the views of young people. A number of statements have been made about the usefulness, appropriateness and necessity of these services yet young people themselves have not been asked. None of these reports included interviews with young people, or service users. It seems that a crucial research variable has been omitted.
>
> (Feaviour 1992: 9)

All those involved in providing youth counselling and information services have highlighted the importance of user feedback, so research that compares user and provider perspectives is particularly relevant and significant.

The results suggested that:

> ... there is no difference between client and provider attitudes and therefore providers of youth counselling and advisory services are fairly 'in touch' with client attitudes and needs. For the dimensions *confidentiality, informality* and *independence* attitudes were similar. This suggests the previous reports emphasis on these dimensions were correct.
>
> (Feaviour 1992: 40)

However results related to specificity of services to young people were less clear. It seems that some young people felt services should be available to all age groups so that they could use them when they felt it was appropriate. For example, many people over 20 do not consider they are young people, and would be happy to use other services if they were available in the same multi-disciplinary way that is available for young people. In a similar way, we have experienced people over 25 who have complained that no services are available for them and felt the age cut-off was very arbitrary.

The results pertaining to confidentiality were not clear. This was because of the different understanding of the word and the lack of definition of the levels of confidentiality that can be offered. Informality was much appreciated and made centres more attractive to young people (Feaviour 1992: 46). It appeared that youth counselling as an independent service was less significant to users than either confidentiality and informality. Although it was clearly important that agencies should be separate from statutory organizations (Feaviour 1992: 47).

To sum up the findings from this research, young people do want a service that is both informal and separate from existing services, one that is confidential and provides accurate information thereby attempting to bridge the gap between informal and professional networks: 'Young people want somewhere that they can turn to and trust without the fear of reprisal from friends or family or being seen as ill or incapable of managing their lives' (Feaviour 1992: 51).

It is also worth noting another piece of research undertaken by Elizabeth Aspinall from Connections in Swindon. She designed, implemented and evaluated a pilot scheme for an annual appraisal for volunteer counsellors which was aimed at monitoring their effectiveness (see Chapter 3). It can equally improve motivation and performance for both the individual and the organization. Appraisal in the context of a youth counselling service is used for developmental purposes, given that unfortunately pay awards and promotion are irrelevant for volunteers. During appraisal, counsellors were able to offer structured feedback to supervisors, the co-ordinator and the organization in general, while experiencing their contributions as valued. They could also influence in a more formal way organizational structures that would directly affect their personal development and involvement in the agency (Aspinall 1993: 10).

Despite predictable difficulties in creating a collaborative appraisal system, considerable learning took place as a result of ongoing enquiry into the best methods for appraisal. In conclusion it was found that: 'For most volunteers the process provided an increased confidence, a more focused sense of direction and a framework for ensuring that their learning needs could be met' (Aspinall 1993: 72). And for the agency and voluntary services in general:

To further the maturation process, and to meet the needs of a considerable number of practitioners, it is important that the counselling world devotes more attention to the establishment of appropriate models of management to support the new breed of workplace counsellors.

(Aspinall 1993: 73)

NATIONAL VOCATIONAL QUALIFICATIONS (NVQs)

The arrival of NVQs in the early nineties is a highly important development in the counselling world, particularly youth counselling. The aims of NVQs are twofold: to recognize and honour the existing skill of workers and volunteers, whose level of competence can be measured against a set of agreed criteria; and second, to provide an alternative training route accessible to a wider group of people. NVQs will not replace the traditional training system of certificate and diploma courses in counselling but would run alongside it. However, in time NVQs and the sterling work of those ensuring their applicability to the counselling world might well affect the style and content of counselling courses.

NVQs are, by their very nature, skill- and competence-based rather than knowledge-based. Their greatest strength lies in their contribution to equal opportunities. Workers who have given their time and enthusiasm, undergone agency training and built up skill, expertise and experience will be able to have their competence assessed and acknowledged. Those who are unable to afford to train in the traditional manner, or who would be excluded from trainings because of their lack of academic achievement would have another route of entry and one which is likely to be agency- rather than personally funded. This should enfranchise a whole body of people including many from traditionally oppressed minorities.

The Advice, Guidance, Counselling and Psychotherapy Lead Body has taken on the task of establishing agreed criteria for competence levels. BAC acted as a broker by asking many of their members to explore and examine their practice and provide information to the lead body. This has been a revealing and largely affirming exercise for the profession.

Talk of NVQs raises much anxiety in the youth counselling world. At present no one knows the cost of the necessary assessments but many fear that they will be so high as to make them prohibitive to smaller agencies. If this is so it is hoped that there will be scope for networking and for bodies such as youth and community departments to undertake assessments for the smaller agencies. Another source of anxiety is the time factor and the fear that already overburdened co-ordinators will have the mammoth task of assessment added to their work loads. Others fear that NVQs will end up being seen as a poor substitute for a 'proper' training. It cannot be denied that counselling, in its anxiety for professional recognition, is highly status-driven and it will take time and goodwill before NVQs are afforded the status they deserve.

Two training routes are likely to develop, perhaps not dissimilar to the Open University's credit system, where a particular level of NVQ could be accepted instead of a foundation course for entry to a diploma. As a competence-based form of assessment of counselling skills, it has a great deal to offer the world of youth counselling; it is hoped that the system will be up and running nationally in the second half of the nineties.

COUNSELLING IN SCHOOLS

The BAC division known as CIE (Counselling in Education) is made up of school counsellors, educational welfare officers, and youth workers. The diversity of this group reflects the different use of counselling in educational settings which can be both formal and more often, informal.

As we have shown, few schools have access to a counsellor, although some areas, for example Dudley, do have a recognized schools counselling service. The schools counselling service in Hemel Hempstead is an example of a service which originated from support services in schools. Pupils who were withdrawn or excluded from school for a variety of reasons were given alternative teaching and work experience. It soon became clear that these pupils' greatest need was to talk and the service changed to provide counselling with five part-time counsellors offering counselling in 13 schools for a total of 40 hours per week. This service is still functioning, although there are now only 10 schools and four counsellors. Each school has between six to eight hours per week counselling time. Contracts are open-ended and pupils have been seen for up to two years, although the norm is six to eight sessions. However, with changes in the system to LMS (Local Management of Schools), schools now have the option to buy in this provision, and may well choose to do so, as it seen by both parents and teachers as a valuable service.

It is surprisingly difficult to know the exact numbers of counsellors who work in schools or schools who employ counsellors. The membership of CIE incorporates a wide spectrum of people reflecting the diversity of counselling provision within schools, as described in Chapter 1. Members meet in regional groups, which provide a support network: this is invaluable to work which is often seen as peripheral to the major focus of the school.

Following the CIE Annual General Meeting in May 1994, further developments have taken place; one important outcome being a decision to develop practice guidelines for counsellors in schools related to issues such as confidentiality. CIE hopes that while the new guidelines will help to clarify the parameters of their role, access to a network of people who are interested in counselling in schools will help to relieve some of the isolation inherent in the work.

As we saw in Chapter 1, counselling in schools is being increasingly valued, although this does not necessarily mean more employment of counsellors. Rather, counselling skills are increasingly used by teachers, who will then use them informally with their students. The Children Act advocated access to counselling in boarding schools, and it is interesting to note that there is to be an increase in schools employing counsellors in the independent sector.

We spoke to counsellors working in schools who offer formal counselling; the problems which emerge seem to be the same as 10 years ago. It remains difficult for pupils to trust the confidentiality of the counsellor when she is constantly seen in the company of classroom teachers. There can be tensions relating to referral; the service needs to be well known and pupils need to be easily able to self-refer. However, although the service must be well known and publicized this is not straightforward either. It is all too easy for the counsellor to be overwhelmed by the response, particularly if there are only a few counselling hours available. The appropriate siting of counselling rooms to ensure relative anonymity is another crucial aspect that often causes problems in schools where space can be at a premium.

Another issue for counsellors working in schools who are not teachers is their relative status. This is often reflected in rates of pay, counsellors frequently being paid less than teaching staff. They also have to consider how to work alongside other support teachers, for instance the behaviour support teachers. In one school the latter worked primarily with groups, while the counsellor worked mainly with individuals. Both might work individually, but in these instances their roles would be clearly defined with, for instance, the teacher focusing on a behavioural aspect. The counsellor would be working in a more holistic way by helping the pupil to explore all relevant aspects of their life.

There is no recognized best method of offering counselling in schools. The issue of confidentiality is crucial. Trust takes time to create and is horribly easy to destroy. Although it is less isolating for the counsellor to be a member of the teaching staff, where this is the case it makes it much more difficult for counselling to appear independent. In many ways the counsellor visiting from outside is a better option for most pupils. This is borne out by the research quoted above (Feaviour 1992), which shows that young people express the greatest concern regarding confidentiality when counselling is in the context of educational establishments.

When schools consider the possibility of employing a counsellor they often have no clear knowledge of what is involved in setting up a counselling service. It is common for counsellors to be expected to liaise closely with year heads, form tutors and other members of the pastoral staff in a way which contradicts the ethos of confidentiality. The job description for a counsellor, in one school, indicated that what was expected was an assessment of the pupil/ client with a view to referral if appropriate. Certainly there was no expectation of ongoing counselling beyond three or four sessions. Perhaps not surprisingly, in the view of this expectation, the counsellor was to be employed for only two hours a week, in a school with over 800 pupils. It could be argued that schemes like this reflect a move towards recognizing the value of counselling. However it is also true that unless there is time for the counsellor to liaise closely with referral agencies, and have at least a degree of confidentiality, schemes such as this can be no more than a token gesture.

A new initiative recently began in a secondary school in Watford, whereby a counsellor from the local young people's counselling and information service went into the school for one afternoon each week to offer individual sessions to students. The school greatly welcomed this connection with the agency, which is situated a long way from the school, and otherwise not easily accessible. Agreements relating to confidentiality, child protection issues and the methods of referral were carefully negotiated before the project began. Inevitably teething problems occurred, with some difficulty over room availability, but so far it appears to be a successful venture. The agency is hoping to try similar projects in other schools but as always funding is the stumbling block.

This project suggests that one alternative way forward for schools is by contracting services from a young people's counselling agency whereby counsellors come into the school. As the Watford example indicates, potentially problematic issues can be agreed beforehand and supervision would be undertaken within the agency. The school benefits by having all the advantages of an in-house service with none of the disadvantages, except perhaps the difficulties for some counsellors of not really understanding the implications of the context.

Pupils could use the service in the school but would know about the young people's agency and could choose to use it directly if they preferred. The school would be paying less and could choose to have different counsellors on different days, rather than just one, depending on their needs. Supervision would be guaranteed and the counsellor would not feel so isolated if they belonged to an existing service where they could share difficulties with other counsellors who also work with young people. There are advantages for the agency too: funding is guaranteed for the hours offered, and less time would be spent promoting the service through outreach work in schools.

PRIVATE PRACTICE

The 1989 Children Act enshrined young people's right to greater levels of self-determination. With rights comes responsibility: young people need education in decision-making. Consequently, social workers are increasingly recognizing the value of counselling for young people, both as part of their enfranchisement and to help them come to terms with their childhood experience and move forward into adulthood. Where no counsellors are employed by Social Services and no youth agencies are available, social workers are buying in the services of private practitioners. Young people are often able to respond positively to a counsellor who is not part of the 'care' world and who offers the young person both confidentiality and impartiality.

There is a particular need for counselling for young people with learning difficulties or with physical disability. As they move out into the community under the community care provision, they often find it hard to adjust to their increasing independence. Here also, where appropriate, some authorities are buying in counselling from private practitioners to support these young people.

It could be argued that this is an expensive extra and perhaps not a justifiable use of public money, but social work teams who have the funds available consider it to be highly cost-effective. It may be that a possible future development for counselling would be the contracting in of counsellors to Social Services and family centres to work not only with young people but also with the wider community.

CONCLUSION

In researching this book we met and talked with many people involved in various capacities with counselling for young people. We were continually impressed by the abundance of commitment, enthusiasm, knowledge and skill. However, with depressing regularity we also met people struggling to survive in a world of shrinking resources often reflected by their poor working conditions and shabby environment. The general consensus that counselling provision for young people is beneficial is not matched by real support and funding. It deserves a higher priority. Society does not seem willing to translate vague support into real action.

The word 'counselling' is loosely used in most documents about the welfare, education and care of young people but little thought is given to the real meaning of the word or its financial implications. It would be easy to become depressed and despondent were it not for the contact with those actively involved in counselling young people who struggle doggedly, and generously give their time and expertise to provide a quality service despite so many odds.

The need for counselling among young people has never been greater. Unemployment, family breakdown, homelessness, poverty and oppression, pressure to succeed matched by lack of real prospects for the future, the allure of drugs and alcohol and difficulties with sexuality all conspire to make the transition from childhood to adulthood difficult and fraught with danger. The old supports of church, family and community are conspicuous by their absence in the lives of many young people. How can those involved in counselling the young ensure that the services they offer continue, let alone expand?

The way forward seems to be by division of labour. Many counsellors are not particularly skilled or indeed interested in fund-raising or even in promoting and selling the service they offer. Young people's counselling projects need to attract a new breed of supporter, those who are more familiar with the ways of Mammon and who would be able to bring their business acumen to bear in a good cause. In the present political climate the only way to survive is to learn to play the game. Good public relations are essential and links with industry and the financial sector are best formed by those who have the skill and experience to make them.

In terms of service delivery, an expansion of the range of people involved is needed. NVQs will partly answer this need as will the development of community-based projects, particularly those serving the black and Asian communities. Projects that really respond to the needs of young people, as defined by young people themselves, will provide both challenge to and the possibility of growth for the counselling establishment, which is sometimes guilty of being a little precious and unwilling to change.

The survival of youth and community departments, which is by no means certain, is fundamental to the future of young people's counselling services. In many areas their support is vital, in terms of staffing, training and premises. Their demise could ring the death knell for many projects connected to them. Unless the political climate changes radically, youth and community departments will do well to maintain their present level of operation and expansion is very unlikely.

A change in the political climate is perhaps the brightest hope of all for young people's counselling services. Since the election of a Conservative government in 1979, it is hard to believe that there has been any real interest in the provision and maintainance of quality services to young people. What we have seen is the dismantling of the safety net previously provided by the social security system and a quite shameful attempt to impose an outdated ideology of the family, which bears no real relation to the situation in which many young people find themselves. At the same time we have seen a dramatic expansion in youth unemployment which has been addressed by a whole series of underfunded initiatives in which young people have had no confidence whatsoever. The election of a government with a real commitment to young people and a willingness to value and listen to those who actually work with them could bring about real change. This commitment would need to be demonstrated by the provision of funding and resources so that workers could concentrate on what they are really good at, the delivery of services to young people, rather than putting endless time and energy into chasing funding. A political climate in which young people are valued instead of blamed for reacting to circumstances over which they have no control and in which prevention and support are rated higher than punishment would not only motivate young people but would raise the morale of people working with them.

The future is not rosy, but nor is it without hope. Young people and their problems are not going to go away and nor are the people who are committed to working with them. Together, as equal partners we have to find the way forward.

Appendix: useful addresses

Alateen
c/o Al-anon Family Group
61 Great Dover Street
London SE1 4YF
0171 403 0888

The Black Therapy Centre
Central Chambers
Ealing Broadway
London W5 2NR
0181 567 7158

British Association for Counselling
1 Regent Place
Rugby
Warwicks CV21 2PJ
01788 578328

Brook Advisory Centres
Education and Publications Unit
153a East Street
London SE17 2FD
0171 708 1234
Sex education for young people.

Centre 33
33 Clarendon Road
Cambridge CB1 1GX
01223 314763

Childline
2nd Floor Royal Mail Building
Studd Street
London NW1 OQN
0171 239 1000

Children's Legal Centre
20 Compton Terrace
London N1 2UN
0171 359 9392
Deals with and has leaflets on the rights of children.

Kidscape
152 Buckingham Palace Road
London SW1W 9TR
0171 730 3300
Leaflets on children's personal safety and bullying.

Mancroft Advice
The Riseborow Trust
Chantry Road
Norwich NR2 1QS
01603 766994

National Youth Agency
17–23 Albion Street
Leicester LE1 6GD
01533 471043
Publishes materials about Information Shops.

No. 5
224 Sackville Street
Reading
Berkshire RG1 1NT
01734 585304

Relateteen
76 Dublin Road
Belfast
BT2 7HP
01232 320709

Signpost
206 Lower High Street
Watford
Herts WD1 2EL
01923 239495

Time Out Project
Caribbean Womens' Association
St Paul & St Silas Church Centre
80 Lozells Rd
Birmingham B19 2TD
0121 515 4198

Yakeen (Asian Women's Network)
1 St Kilda's Road
Harrow HA1 1QA
0181 427 6796

Youth Access
1–2 Taylors Yard
67 Alderbrook Road
London SW12
Membership organization of young people's counselling and information services.

References

Antournis, G. (1977) 'Counselling in the mid-seventies', *The Counsellor*. In Hooper, R. and Lang, P., *Pastoral Care*, 6(2): 28.

Aspinall, E. (1993) 'Creative appraisal: or crime and punishment'. Bristol University: M.Sc. dissertation.

Association for Student Counselling (1992) *Requirements for Accreditation*, Rugby: ASC.

Bailey, C. and Philips, M. (1990) *Counselling Young Adults*. London: Thames Publications.

Bond, T. (1992) 'Ethical issues in counselling in education', *British Journal of Guidance and Counselling*, 20(1): 51–63.

Bond, T. (1993) *Standards of Ethics for Counselling in Action*. London: Sage Publications.

British Association of Counselling (1992) *Code of Ethics and Practice*. Rugby: BAC.

British Psychological Society (1985) *A Code of Conduct for Psychologists*. Leicester: BPS.

Childline (1993) *Annual Report*. London: Childline.

Cross, W.E. (1980) 'Models of psychological nigrescence: a literature review', in Jones, R.L. (ed.), *Black Psychology*. New York: Harper and Row.

Daws, P.P. (1973) 'Mental health and education: counselling as a prophylaxis', *British Journal of Guidance and Counselling*, 1(2): 2–10.

Egan, G. (1975) *The Skilled Helper*. Monterey, CA: Brooks-Cole.

Ellis, A. (1977) *Handbook of Rational Emotive Therapy*. New York: Springer Verlag.

European Community Action Programme (1985) *Transitions of Young People from Education to Adulthood and Working Life*. Brussels: EEC.

Feaviour, K. (1992) 'The attitudes of clients and providers of youth counselling and advisory agencies toward the dimensions confidentiality, informality, specificity to youth and independence'. Roehampton Institute: M.Sc. dissertation.

Francis, S. and Ali, O. (1993) *Black Therapy*. London: Village Communications.

Galloway, D. (1990) *Pupil Welfare and Counselling*. London: Longman.

Hare, J. and Hare, N. (1985) *Bringing the Black Boy to Manhood: The Passage*. San Francisco, CA: Black Think Tank.

Her Majesty's Inspectors (1989) *Youth Counselling Services*. Stanmore: Department of Education and Science.

HMSO (1969) *Youth and Community Work in the 1970's*. London: HMSO.

Hooper, R. and Lang, P. (1988) 'Counselling revisited', *Pastoral Care*, 6(2): 27–32.

Jacobs, M. (1988) *Psychodynamic Counselling in Action*. London: Sage.

Karenga, N. (1980) *Kawaida Theory: An Introductory Outline*. Inglewood, CA: Kawaida Publications.

Law, B. (1975) 'The concept of counselling', in Vaughn, T. (ed) *Concepts of Counselling*. London: Bedford Square Press.

Lawton, A. (1980) *Confidentiality in NAYPCAS Information*, Leaflet C8. Leicester: Youth Counselling Development Unit.

Lawton, A. (1985) 'Youth counselling', *British Journal of Guidance and Counselling*, 13(1): 35–48.

McDonald, E. (1990) *The Information Shop Specification*. Leicester: National Youth Agency.

Maguire, U. (1975) 'The school counsellor as therapist', *British Journal of Guidance and Counselling*, 3(2): 160–70.

Milner, P. (1980) *Counselling in Education*. Trowbridge: Redwood Burn.

Mosely, J. (1993) 'Is there a place for counselling in schools?', *Journal of the BAC*, 4(2).

Murgatroyd, S. (1983) *Counselling and Helping*. London: Methuen.

National Association of Mental Health (1970) *School Counselling*. London: NAMH.

National Association of Youth Counselling and Advisory Services (1984) *Policy Document*. Leicester: NAYPCAS.

National Youth Bureau (1990) *The Local Youth Bureaux Initiative: A Consultation Report*. Leicester: NYB.

Nelson-Jones, R. (1987) 'DOSIE: a five stage model for problem management counselling and helping', *British Journal of Guidance and Counselling*. In Meredith, A., 'Comprehensive Counselling: One pupil's Integration' *BJGC* 21(1) January 1993: 95–105.

Noonan, E. (1983) *Counselling Young People*. London: Methuen.

Priestley, P., McGuire, J., Flegg, D., Helmsley, V. and Welham, D. (1978) *Social Skills and Personal Problem Solving*. London: Tavistock.

Sawyer, A. (1983) *Report on Agencies in the Metropolitan Area of London*. London (unpublished).

Stephens, J. and Scutt, N. (1993) *Child Advocacy Service*. Plymouth: Youth Enquiry Service.

Thompson, A. (1982) *Experience and Participation: Youth Service Review*. London: HMSO.

Thomson, H. (1993) *A Measure of Good Practice*. Leicester: Youth Access.

Tyler, M. (1978) *Advisory and Counselling Services for Young People*. DHSS Research Report No. 1. London: HMSO.

Van Deurzen-Smith, E. (1988) *Existential Counselling in Practice*. London: Sage.

White, P. (1993) *Information Shops in Action*. Leicester: Youth Work Press.

World Health Organization (1978) *Summary Report*. London: WHO.

Yalom, I. (1931) *Existential Psychotherapy*. New York: Basic Books.

Youth Access (1994) *Code of Ethics and Practice*. Leicester: Youth Access.

Index

COUNSELLING FOR WOMEN

Janet Perry

Although few in number, organizations which provide counselling services for women have had a tremendous impact on our current understanding of women's psychology and the issues women explore in counselling. Through her examination of these organizations, Janet Perry highlights the unique emphasis they place on the importance of how services are provided and their exploration of the dynamics of the working relationships of women counsellors. The organizations included in the book range from Women's Aid to Women's Therapy Centres and their services are considered in the context of counselling women. The study shows that through a self-reflexive examination of their organizational processes, these agencies have come to a greater understanding of the ways in which women working with women create non-hierarchical and cooperative endeavours, much needed in our individualistic and competitive society. The book illustrates the conflicts that arise when both modes seek to exist within one organization – Family Service Units – and the struggle all the agencies have to legitimize these ways of working to a male dominated system from which funding is often sought. Recommended reading for all those involved in counselling and psychotherapy, this book illustrates some of the practical outcomes of these alternative working models.

Contents

The development of counselling in women's organizations – Counselling in women's organizations – The practice of counselling women – Specific issues in counselling women – Professional relationships in counselling for women – Critique of counselling for women – References – Index.

128pp   0 335 19034 0 (Paperback)

COUNSELLING IN INDEPENDENT PRACTICE

Gabrielle Syme

This book demonstrates and reflects the care and responsibility that must be taken by anyone considering counselling in independent practice. It is a thoughtful book based upon the experience of a skilled and well-trained practitioner who has set her own standards high. For anyone contemplating setting up in private or independent practice as a counsellor or psychotherapist it offers an excellent model. It explores in depth the practical, ethical and personal issues that should be considered before taking such a major step. Concluding with a critique of private and independent practice, the book makes a powerful contribution to the current debate about the difference between the minimum standards set by Codes of Ethics and Practice for counsellors and what is good practice. The professional practitioner will recognize the points of discussion raised by the author. For this group, the book provides a yardstick by which to assess the quality of service they provide and the relationship that they maintain with their clients. With its useful exploration of this relationship, the book will also be of interest to anyone considering counselling or psychotherapeutic help, and those referring patients or colleagues.

Contents
The development of counselling in independent practice – Counselling in independent practice – The practice of counselling in independent practice – Specific issues in counselling in independent practice – Professional relationships in counselling in independent practice – A critique of counselling in independent practice – Appendices – References – Index.

160pp   0 335 19049 9 (Paperback)

COUNSELLING IN THE VOLUNTARY SECTOR

Nicholas Tyndall

Nicholas Tyndall has drawn upon his extensive experience of counselling and training in personal and family organizations to provide a comprehensive picture of the voluntary sector. In his clear, accessible style, he outlines the beginnings of counselling in Britain and charts the development of the growing number of specialist and generic agencies.

The book is written in the firm belief that the voluntary sector can combine what is best in the amateur and the professional. Its scope and practices are explored. Methods of selection, training and supervision of counsellors are compared, and the challenges facing staff and management committees are examined. The book highlights the strengths and weaknesses of voluntary counselling, and identifies the need to improve equal opportunities, fill new gaps and develop inter-agency collaboration. The author has harsh words for public bodies which have high expectations of volunteers but are not prepared to meet the cost. He offers helpful advice for existing agencies and those wanting to improve their personal services; and guidance to individuals who are interested in becoming counsellors.

Contents

The development of counselling in the voluntary sector – Voluntary agencies – The practice of counselling in the voluntary sector – Specific issues in counselling in the voluntary sector – Professional relationships in counselling in the voluntary sector – A critique of counselling in the voluntary sector – References – Index.

160pp   0 335 19027 8 (Paperback)